Third Party Blues

More than many areas of American politics research, studies of minor party competition and success are often overly driven by normative concerns backed by little empirical scrutiny. This concise book presents a concerted effort to analyze the barriers in election law, such as ballot access restrictions and single-member districts with a plurality rule, that prevent third parties from gaining a durable hold in American politics.

Rather than trudge through yet another history of third parties in America or polemical arguments for minor party inclusion, Schraufnagel provides empirical grounding for the claims of third party backers. This thoughtful analysis demonstrates that the inclusion of third parties improves electoral participation rates and that third party involvement in the legislative process is linked to landmark legislative productivity. In the end, the work provides thoughtful suggestions on the types of reforms that would lead to greater third party success in American elections.

Scot Schraufnagel is an Assistant Professor in the Department of Political Science at Northern Illinois University. His research and teaching focuses on political parties, elections, and legislatures in the United States, with an emphasis on promoting a civil, representative, and effective governing process. Schraufnagel has been recognized for teaching excellence and has been published in a number of leading political science journals.

FR-47500

Controversies in Electoral Democracy and Representation
Matthew J. Streb, Series Editor

The Routledge series *Controversies in Electoral Democracy and Representation* presents cutting edge scholarship and innovative thinking on a broad range of issues relating to democratic practice and theory. An electoral democracy, to be effective, must show a strong relationship between representation and a fair open election process. Designed to foster debate and challenge assumptions about how elections and democratic representation *should* work, titles in the series present a strong but fair argument on topics related to elections, voting behavior, party and media involvement, representation, and democratic theory.

Rethinking American Electoral Democracy, 2nd Edition
Matthew J. Streb

Third Party Blues
The Truth and Consequences of Two-Party Dominance
Scot Schraufnagel

Forthcoming:

Helping America Vote
The Limits of Election Reform
Martha E. Kropf and David C. Kimball

In Defense of Politicians
Stephen K. Medvic

Third Party Blues

The Truth and Consequences of Two-Party Dominance

Scot Schraufnagel

Routledge
Taylor & Francis Group

NEW YORK AND LONDON

First published 2011
by Routledge
711 Third Avenue, New York, NY 10017

Simultaneously published in the UK
by Routledge
2 Park Square, Milton Park, Abingdon, Oxon OX14 4RN

Routledge is an imprint of the Taylor & Francis Group, an informa business

Library of Congress Cataloging-in-Publication Data
Schraufnagel, Scot.
Third party blues : the truth and consequences of two party
dominance / Scot Schraufnagel.
p. cm.—(Controversies in electoral democracy and
representation)
1. Political parties—United States. 2. Third parties (United
States politics) 3. Opposition (Political science)—United States.
4. Political participation—United States. 5. United States—Politics
and government—1989–1. Title.
JK2261.S36 2011
324.273—dc22   2010043738

ISBN: 978-0-415-88158-6 (hbk)
ISBN: 978-0-415-88159-3 (pbk)
ISBN: 978-0-203-84780-0 (ebk)

Typeset in ITC Galliard
by RefineCatch Limited, Bungay, Suffolk, UK

Printed and bound in the United States of America on acid-free paper
by Walsworth Publishing Company, Marceline, MO

SUSTAINABLE
FORESTRY
INITIATIVE

Certified Sourcing
www.sfiprogram.org

The SFI label applies to the text stock.

To my wife who put up with me going back to school twice in the first ten years of our marriage and our two lovely daughters, Hillary and Autumn.

Contents

Figures

Tables

Preface

I was born in 1959 and socialized to support the Republican Party by my business-owner father. But, my maternal grandfather was a pro-union Democrat. I recall my father defending Richard Nixon, but I also remember his younger brother saying good things about John F. Kennedy and I was confused. As a young boy of about six, I got out the encyclopedia one day and tried to show my Democrat grandfather that all of the famous presidents had been Republican. The encyclopedia listed Thomas Jefferson as a Republican and neither grandpa nor I knew that this was not the same Republican Party in existence in the 1960s. I continued supporting the Republican Party up through most of Watergate in the early 1970s. Those of you that can remember know it became very difficult to be a vocal supporter of Richard Nixon in 1973–74. Yet I was. I remember arguing with classmates about the virtues of President Nixon and biting my pillow at night screaming in my head—"burn the tapes," "burn the tapes!" A reference to the tape recordings that were found to exist and likely contained information that would find Nixon culpable of "high crimes and misdemeanors," grounds for impeachment.

As an 18-year-old college freshman in 1977 I was convinced that we needed a third party in American politics. Jimmy Carter was president and he was advocating for a Selective Service System (SSS) that would require 18–26 year olds to register with the national government so that information could be maintained on those potentially eligible for military conscription. Vietnam was very fresh in my mind and I had begun to view military violence with a great deal of suspicion. I vaguely sensed the crippled Republican Party (post-Watergate) would not do much to stop the Carter initiative from becoming reality. So I joined the Revolutionary Communist Youth Brigade (RCYB), which was planning to demonstrate against the selective service program. The RCYB rhetoric also entailed the overthrow of the national government, which seemed a bit harsh to me, but at least they expressed a fresh point of view and I liked that. When the police showed up at a RCYB rally at Kent State, which was intended as a protest against the planned construction of a gymnasium on the site where students had lost their lives five years earlier, I broke from the formation of RCYB supporters and decided this kind of violence was not for me either. Further disillusionment ensued. I quit the RCYB and decided to try to forget about politics for awhile.

Along came John Anderson, independent candidate for president in 1980. My political fire was ignited and I thought the answer had been found. At least I hoped so, and decided to get active again, joining Anderson's political campaign in Madison, Wisconsin as a volunteer. I learned very quickly, however, that it was not going to be a fair contest. Anderson was having difficulty getting his name on the ballot in many states. How could this be? Surely, the rules for ballot access must be the same for everyone. Moreover, I sensed the media was not giving Anderson the same chance of winning as the other candidates, which happened to be accurate journalism but I did not see it that way. I knew enough about human nature that if the media kept referencing Anderson's candidacy as a "long shot" and his electoral chances as "slim" that this would depress the enthusiasm of potential supporters. Who was going to vote for someone who was being portrayed as a loser before he even got started? When Ronald Reagan won handily in 1980 I became convinced that the political system was broke, and vowed to leave the country as soon as I could. I am not sure why, I just wanted out.

Upon graduation from college, I joined the Peace Corps and low and behold wound up working for President Ronald Reagan. I did succeed in leaving the country but not under the conditions I had imagined. As a Peace Corps in the early 1980s, I got to experience firsthand the selective austerity measures of the Reagan Administration. Peace Corps stipends, about 30 dollars per month, were not to be increased in 1983 and Sierra Leone, West African volunteers would need to share one doctor with volunteers in other West African nations. Previously, each West African nation had its own Peace Corps doctor. I somehow managed to successfully complete Peace Corps service having survived several bouts of malaria and the budget cuts, and was traveling back to the United States when I learned that Reagan was getting re-elected in a landslide. What had he done that was worthy of so much support, I was wondering? I was not impressed with Walter Mondale and I could see why he might lose—I just could not understand how a Hollywood actor with less than impressive film credentials could have won—again! There must be other individuals who could do a better job than Reagan. In a country as large and as well-educated as the United States of America, there must be more than Ronald Reagan and Walter Mondale to choose from. Are these two really the best we have to offer? Subsequently, I have pondered that same query it seems endlessly in regards to races to fill governorships, United States Senate and House seats, and races for state and local government offices.

Fast forward to the future and what are the realistic prospects for third party candidates in the United States in the 21st century? Truth be told, the diagnosis for third parties and independent candidates in 2011 forward, under existing election laws, is ruin. The only saving grace is that death will often come quickly. Why is this so? Can it be that the Democratic and Republican

Parties continue to represent everything and anything good and they are all anyone could ever possibly want in a political party? Interestingly, a recent Wall Street Journal–NBC poll found that 31 percent of Americans agreed with the statement, "The two-party system is seriously broken, and the country needs a third party." The National Election Study (NES) conducted by the University of Michigan routinely finds about a third of Americans do not immediately identify with either the Republican or Democratic Parties. In states that require you to join one of the two major political parties in order to vote in party primaries, there have always been significant numbers of people who choose not to do so, even when it means they will be shut out of the candidate selection process. This is neither new news nor old news. Since the early days of the country, and still today, there is public sentiment in favor of third parties. Successful and sustained third parties electoral achievement, however, has been and is missing.

If one did not know better, one might imagine the system is rigged to promote two-party dominance. Oh sure, an occasional third party or independent candidate wins a race now and then, but in terms of sustained-broad third party achievement it has really never existed in the United States. The last time a third party candidate became president it was Abraham Lincoln, representing the Republicans, in 1860. But this party was only six years old at the time and it very quickly, even before 1860, became one of the two dominant political parties. In Chapter 4, I will look to isolate the influence third parties have had on policy making in the United States. In doing so it will be necessary to identify a time period when third parties had a reasonable level of electoral success in national politics in order to provide a practical test. To do this it will be necessary to go back before the 76th Congress (1939–40). There has been no real third party representation since. Even in the earlier era, third party electoral success was relatively short lived and never amounted to any kind of permanent opposition to the partisan duopoly that has come to shape the legislative process and politics generally in the United States.

This book seeks to tell the story about what blocks meaningful third party opposition in the United States. A primary assumption driving the work is that a high level of political party competition is what defines quality elections and a competent electoral system. Continuing down the assumptive thread, the research holds that competitive-quality elections prompt a more engaged and representative legislative discourse and this, in turn, leads to higher-quality public policies. These assumptions are not original and have been effectively argued by competent scholars and third party advocates for some time. That is good news from my perspective. I will not need to reinvent theory used to justify the value of more meaningful electoral competition, nor the worth of consequential third party competition.

What then is the value of yet another book on the dismal plight of third parties in the United States? Others have written about how the electoral deck of cards is stacked against third parties, and still others expressly advocate for third party inclusion in government. The problem with these earlier works is that they have not yet accomplished what they set out to do, make the American public more aware that the grounds for third party failure is a "stacked deck" and that without fundamental change in existing election laws there is no hope for third party success.

In the course of research for this book, I have tried every imaginable way to convince myself that I was wrong. I tried to convince myself that third parties only need easier ballot access; that third parties do not really stimulate public interest in politics; and that third parties when they have been successful have not had any meaningful influence on important legislative accomplishments. As a political scientist I am trained to try to prove my pet theories wrong. In this effort I have failed miserably.

Hence, the purpose of the book is twofold. First, to provide empirical evidence of the factors preventing third parties from being successful in the United States. Not just conjecture or speculation about why third parties fail, but hard evidence born of rigorous empirical testing that explains the real cause of third party failure. Second, the book intends to provide empirical grounding and evidence to support the value of third parties in terms of higher-quality legislative productivity and a more engaged and politically active public. To date, strong theoretical arguments have been made in support of third party inclusion in the United States and others have readily recognized that there are considerable electoral barriers for third parties to navigate. What has not been accomplished is a comprehensive statement concerning the true cause of third party misfortune and the measureable real-world consequences of two-party dominance.

Acknowledgments

I have been blessed with two mentors in my still relatively short academic career. Jeffery Mondak and Lawrence C. Dodd have been instrumental in the development of the ideas contained within this book. In particular, early work with Mondak helped to shape my thinking about partisan difference. Our earlier co-authored work found that the two major parties are distinct but fail to represent the full spectrum of ideological viewpoints. My ongoing work with Dodd continues to influence the way I think about legislative process and legislative accomplishment. Professor Dodd was particularly instrumental in the development of the theory regarding the paradoxical quality of legislative conflict found in Chapter 4.

I could not have completed work on this project without the dedicated research assistance received from students at Northern Illinois University. The extent to which each of the students listed below contributed varies, yet, each one was instrumental. I am listing the names alphabetically to avoid trying to make qualitative judgments about whose input was most valuable. The bottom line, the work would not have been completed during the summer of 2010 without the assistance of Austin Bergen, Ben Bingle, James Carter, Jenn Soss, and Matthew Venaas. There is one additional student that needs to be mentioned. Kerri Milita provided invaluable assistance over a period of approximately three years while we were both at the University of Central Florida. She assisted in the development of most of the original data bases employed in the book. In some instances the student will pass the teacher in both knowledge and accomplishment. I am certain that will be the case with Kerri.

Reader's Note

Throughout this book the term "third party" will be used. Of course, in many instances there have been fourth and fifth political parties running for elected office. The term "third party" is used generically to refer to any political party organization other than the two dominant political parties. "Third party" is not used, however, to refer to independent candidates running for public office or independent politicians who have managed to hold public office. These individuals will be referred to as "independents," and the state they reside in or represent will be noted. In addition, the term "non-major party candidate" will be used; particularly, in Chapters 2 and 3 that test the role election rules play in deciding the fate of candidates. The term "non-major party candidate" includes members of third parties and independent candidates or anyone receiving votes that are not a member of one of the two major political parties.

Throughout the volume there will be reference to the actual number of third party members that have served in Congress or state legislatures. Different historical accounts often vary when reporting third party representation. This occurs for two justifiable reasons. First, some historical accounts will use the number of seats won by a third party while other sources count the actual number of people who have served under the third party label. When a third party member of Congress has died or leaves office for any reason and the vacancy is subsequently filled by a different third party member, the level of third party representation will vary in different historical accounts. Second, third party candidates have often won office as fusion candidates where the individual represents both a third party and one of the major political parties. In these instances, there can also be discrepancies in reporting the level of third party representation. Some accounts choose to regard the individual as representing the major party and others count the candidate as a third party representative.

When stating levels of third party representation in the United States Congress, this work uses the numbers provided by the Clerk of the United States House of Representatives website and the Secretary of the United States

Senate website. References to third party representation in state legislatures are obtained from Michael J. Dubin, *Party Affiliations in the State Legislatures: A Year by Year Summary, 1796–2006* (Jefferson, NC: McFarland and Company), 2007; and cross referenced with data from *The Book of the States* published by the Council of State Governments, Lexington, Kentucky.

Chapter 1

The Case for Third Party Representation

No member of an organized third party has gained a seat in the United States Congress (House and Senate) for over 50 years. Ever wondered why? Few people realize it, but there is very minimal third party representation in state legislatures either. In 2008, a total of 20 out of a possible 7382 legislative seats in the 99 chambers of the 50 state legislatures were occupied by non-major party representatives.[1] More specifically, there were three senators and 17 members of state lower chambers. Of these 20, only 11 were actual members of an organized third political party, and of these 11, six were from one political party in one state: the Progressive Party in the state of Vermont. And now that you know, have you ever wondered why there are so few third party representatives in state legislatures or why Democrats and Republicans dominate electoral politics in the United States today? Is it the case that Democrats and Republicans represent everything—and anything—that anyone could possibly want in a political party? Are the two mainstream political parties just that good?

Reasonable students of politics are likely to recognize the assumption that the two major political parties in the United States are "just that good" is somehow incomplete. In public opinion polls conducted by Columbia Broadcasting System (CBS) News, in May 2010, 55 percent of respondents had an unfavorable opinion of the Republican Party and 54 percent had an unfavorable view of the Democratic Party.[2] The "favorable" ratings were equally unimpressive. Thirty-three percent viewed the Republican Party favorably and 37 percent viewed the Democrats favorably;[3] hardly, a ringing endorsement of the big two political parties.

Some might imagine that the reason for the lack of third party success in the United States is that Democrats and Republicans have a monopoly on good ideas. Perhaps third parties do not have any reasonable policy prescriptions that can be taken seriously. Yet, in 1992, when the non-major party presidential candidate Ross Perot suggested that we did not need "free" trade as much as we needed "fair" trade, the Republican Party was more than willing to take up this issue and use it as part of their campaign advertising in the 1994 midterm elections. Similarly, when Perot suggested that the nation's annual deficits were unacceptable and that the nation's total debt was spiraling out of control, newly elected Democratic president Bill Clinton knew he would need to act quickly in 1993, resulting in the country's first balanced budget near the end of his second term. The *de facto* leader of the Democrat Party, President Clinton, seemed to think this non-major party idea, a balanced budget, was a good one. In Chapter 4, there will be considerable evidence presented which suggests third parties, historically, have had lots of good ideas. Ideas such as a minimum wage, a woman's right to vote, and the direct election of United States senators; ideas that subsequently were supported by one or both of the two major political parties and became law.

Still others might imagine the reason third parties do not fare well in American elections is that they do not produce quality candidates, are not well-organized, or do not have sufficient resources to compete with Democrats and Republicans. These speculations about third party failure would be more reasonable. Political scientists often measure candidate "quality" by virtue of previous experience running for and winning elected office.[4] For instance, if a candidate for the United States House of Representatives had previously served as a state senator or state representative, that individual would be classified as a "quality" candidate: one that has a reasonable chance of winning. It is often the case that third party candidates do not have this quality or characteristic. In recent years, the most visible third parties, nationwide—the Constitution Party, the Green Party, the Libertarian Party, and the Reform Party—have had difficulty recruiting candidates with previous experience winning elections. In 2008, there was only one member from any of these four national third parties holding a state legislative seat, suggesting little "quality" or winning electoral experience to draw on if the goal were to hold a seat in the national Congress.

In addition to their lack of quality candidates it is almost certainly the case that today's third parties are not as well organized as either the Democratic or Republican Parties. Moreover, it is a reality that today's third parties do not have the same financial resources as the two major political parties. Lack of candidate identity and the lack of third party resources are certainly part of the explanation for third party electoral failure. The problem with these explanations for the lack of third party success is not their accuracy. Instead, the issue is what came first: the lack of electoral success or the lack of identity and resources? One can hardly expect people to want to contribute money to candidates and political parties with no reasonable chance of winning. Moreover, with no track record of electoral success it is not surprising that third party staffers find it difficult to sustain organizational momentum.

Dim electoral prospects and minimal campaign resources run together; this much is not particularly newsworthy. What is interesting to consider, however, is the prospect that sustained failure is causing inadequate resources and not the other way around. Given the over 200-year history of political parties in the United States and long-standing two-party dominance, one has to imagine that there must have been instances when third parties would have had the necessary resources to produce a viable and consistent electoral option for voters. Yet this has never happened. Table 1.1 exhibits the third parties that have managed to obtain representation in the United States House of Representatives and the years of their success. One can easily recognize that sustained achievement has been elusive, practically non-existent, and that electoral accomplishment of any kind since the mid-20th century is absent. The same story can be told for the United States Senate. Thus, given the lack of

Table 1.1 Third Party Representation in the United States House of Representatives[a]

Party Name	Years of Representation	Congress w/Max. Representation	Max. Representation
Anti-Masonic Party	1829–41	23rd (1833–35)	25/240–10.4%
Nullifier Party	1831–39	23rd (1833–35)	9/240–3.8%
Law and Order Party (of R.I.)	1843–45	28th (1843–45)	2/223–0.9%
American Republican Party	1845–51	29th (1845–47)	6/228–2.6%
American "Know-Nothing" Party	1855–61	34th (1859–61)	51/234–21.8%
Anti-Lecompton Party	1859–61	34th (1859–61)	8/234–3.4%
Unionist Party	1861–67	37th (1861–63)	28/183–15.3%
Constitutional Union Party	1861–63	37th (1861–63)	2/183[b]–1.1%
Unconditional Union Party	1863–67	38th (1863–65)	16/184–8.7%
Conservative Party[c]	1867–71	41st (1869–71)	5/243–2.1%
Liberal Republicans	1871–75	43rd (1873–75)	4/292–1.4%
Nationals (Greenbacks)	1879–85	46th (1879–81)	13/293–4.4%
Re-Adjusters	1883–85	48th (1883–85)	4/325–1.2%
Populist Party	1891–1905	55th (1897–99)	22/357–6.2%
Silver Party	1893–1901	Never more than one member.	
Silver Republican Party	1897–1903	55th (1897–99)	3/357–0.8%
Socialist Party	1911–29[d]	Never more than one member.	
Prohibition Party	1915–21	Never more than one member.	
Progressive Party (Roosevelt)	1913–19	63rd (1913–15)	9/435–2.1%
Progressive Party (La Follette)	1935–47	75th (1937–38)	8/435–1.8%
American Labor Party	1939–51	Never more than one member.	

Notes
a Not included are Independents (without political party affiliation), Independent Democrats, and Independent Republicans. The maximum number of independent members in Congress occurred in the 36th Congress (1859–61). Specifically, there were seven Independent Democrats out of a total of 239 members, representing about 2.9 percent of the chamber.
b The size of the House of Representatives decreased during the Civil War.
c There have been several different political parties in the history of the United States that have gone by the name the Conservative Party.
d With two gaps, or Congresses, where there was no member.

sustained third party electoral success, and no accomplishment in recent years, it should be no surprise that it is difficult for third parties to attract sufficient contributions. A long history of electoral failure has to work against the opportunity of third parties to attract the requisite resources to be successful.

If it is the case that a history of poor electoral performance makes it difficult for third parties to attract significant electoral resources, then the lack of electoral success came first. The causal arrow goes from the lack of success to the lack of resources. Therefore, it is not entirely fair to say that a lack of quality candidates and electioneering assets causes third party failure. After all, third party failure predates the modern era of minimal third party assets.

There are certainly exceptions to the rule. There have been instances when the lack of electoral success has not swayed a non-major party candidate from marshalling significant resources to make a reasonable run for public office. Witness the Perot candidacy mentioned above. When Ross Perot ran for president in 1992, a third party candidate had not won the presidency since the election of 1860. That year Illinois Republican Abraham Lincoln managed to receive a plurality of the popular votes and a majority of the Electoral College in a five-person race with a political party system disrupted and factionalized by the Civil War. Yet, in 1992, Perot brought ample resources to the task of campaigning for the highest office in the land. Over 130 years of third party failure in presidential contests did not convince Perot it was a mistake to run, or spend in the millions.

There has been other undeterred, and successful, third party or independent candidates in recent years. Nearly everyone knows the story of Jesse "the Body" Ventura and his successful bid to become governor of Minnesota. Angus King, an independent candidate without party affiliation, Lowell Weicker a member of the "A Connecticut Party," and Walter Hickel a member of the "Alaskan Independence Party" all won their state's top political office since 1990. Each of these instances, however, comes with unique circumstances. The candidates either had significant name recognition, previously held office as a member of one of the two major political parties, or had considerable amounts of their own financial resources. In each instance, the non-major party gubernatorial candidates did not need to establish name recognition or rely wholly on public campaign contributions. Without these special circumstances these non-major party gubernatorial candidates would have undoubtedly found things much more difficult.[5] Furthermore, in each of the instances, the actual third parties involved have since diminished in significance. In the case of Perot, who did not win with resources on par with the major party candidates, his crippled Reform Party struggles along in the early years of the 21st century without sufficient resources to realistically challenge Democrats and Republicans.

Third party electoral failure seems to prompt additional third party frustration, submission, and disappointment, and if the lack of electoral success predates the lack of resources, then it is not fair to suggest that the lack of resources causes third party failure. Third parties were failing before the present-day resource distribution was defined. Moreover, when popular and successful third party candidates appear, perhaps winning an election or two, this effort is not sustained. A short period of time passes and we are back to just two dominant political parties (see Table 1.1).

If one can accept that Democrats and Republicans do not give us all the meaningful electoral choice we desire and that third party failure is not caused by a lack of good third party ideas, then there is obviously something else causing the problem. Lack of resources is surely a dilemma, but the lack of sustained success precedes the compromised resources and organizational competence of today's third parties. What then is the cause of a lack of third party success? Perhaps election rules and procedures, written by the major parties, have made it difficult for third parties to be successful? This question is the focus of Chapters 2 and 3 of this book. The short answer is: yes, election rules are the problem. Sorting out which electoral arrangements (rules) are most responsible is a more difficult question. The next chapters will provide a reasonable test and a subsequent answer.

But, before examining the election rules that cause third parties to appear and then disappear, it makes sense to first explore whether there is any advantage to viable third parties. It must be clear that there are benefits to be gained from having more than two electoral options, and minimal drawbacks. Reasonable and competent scholars have made claims suggesting that a two-party dominant political party system is preferable, especially when compared to multi-party democracies, and these arguments must be addressed head on.

In particular, many comparative political scientists and citizens grumble about the instability of coalition governments. Coalition governments become necessary when no political party holds a majority of the seats in a nation's legislature, a common occurrence in multi-party democracies. Others question the value of giving a say to minor parties representing ideologically extreme issue positions. These arguments cannot be ignored and the remainder of this chapter will address these concerns.

First, the issue of the representative quality of the two major political parties in the United States will be examined. Do Democrats and Republicans adequately perform the job of representing the broad range of interests that exists in the United States? Do they cover all the bases? Then, the arguments outlined above and others which have been made to defend two-party dominance will be examined. Of particular concern is that two-party dominance should be compared with all possible alternatives and not just contrasted with a pure proportional representation system. In a proportional system, political parties receive representation based on their level of electoral support, so that a party with 5 percent of the vote might secure 5 percent of the seats in the legislature. This can cause lots of political parties to be represented in the legislature. When individuals argue in favor of a two-party dominant system, they often contrast it with a proportional system with lots of parties.

This first chapter concludes with a synopsis of each of the remaining chapters and outlines the objective of each. Keeping in mind the title of the book, the goal throughout will be to uncover the truth about why two parties have dominated United States electoral politics, but also the consequences of the Democratic/Republican duopoly.

Democrats, Republicans, and Representation

The former governor of Alabama and American Independent Party candidate for president, George Wallace, once proclaimed there "is not a dime's worth of difference" between the two major political parties that dominate elections in the United States. Ralph Nader, consumer advocate and former Green Party presidential candidate, has suggested that voters are asked to choose between "look-a-like candidates from two-parties vying to see who takes the marching orders from their campaign paymasters and their future employers."[6] Still again, Pat Buchanan, television personality and former Reform Party presidential candidate, has chided that the two major political parties "are two wings of the same bird of prey."[7] What is particularly interesting about the comments made by the three former third party presidential candidates is that each is voicing annoyance over the lack of a meaningful difference between the two major political parties but on completely different grounds. In the case of Governor Wallace, he was frustrated by Democratic and Republican duplicity on the issue of states' rights. Ralph Nader, for his part, is suggesting that both major parties are too beholden to corporate or business interests and Pat Buchanan feels neither party is sufficiently fiscally or morally conservative. In each instance the two major parties did not provide sufficiently distinct representation to satisfy these presidential hopefuls. One must imagine the people who voted for these third party candidates, and others who might have voted for them if they thought there was a reasonable chance they would win, also felt that the major party candidates were not adequate.

Anthony Downs, a well-respected scholar, suggested that candidates in a two-party dominant political system will not differ much from one another, on average.[8] His "convergence theory" suggests that those who run for public office in competitive electoral districts will rationally moderate their policy stands and move to the policy position of the median voter. This is particularly the case in single-member districts under plurality rule, or the type of election used in the vast majority of contests for state and national offices in the United States. Single-member districts, just like it sounds, mean there is only one member elected from each constituency or district. Plurality rule implies whoever gets the most votes wins, regardless of whether their vote total represents a majority of the votes cast. Under these election rules, candidates must hug the ideological middle ground. There will not be any prize for finishing second or effectively representing citizens with either strong liberal or conservative issue positions. Those with strong views will not hold the median preference in the district. Instead, the winning candidate and political party, under these election rules, must gravitate toward the center. If one pays close attention to election campaigns, it is not difficult to notice Democratic Party candidates sounding more like Republicans and vice-versa as Election Day draws near.

A popular textbook on American government read by college freshmen argues, "One of the most familiar observations about American politics is that the two major parties try to be all things to all people."[9] John Kingdom, in his classic study of legislator voting behavior, found that the leaders of the two major political parties in Congress often seek "consensus" on policy matters.[10] Scholars also argue that because of libertarian and populist sentiments in both major political parties, there are overlapping divisions within the partisan and ideological foundations of the American party system.[11] In all, these arguments are suggesting that representation may be compromised in a two-party dominant political system. First, the parties may not distinguish themselves. Second, there is the possibility of collusion as leaders of the two major parties seek consensus. Last, there are overlapping divisions which may cause confusion in the voting public as individuals try to understand which of the two parties is truly for more states' rights, which is willing to take on corporate America, and which can be trusted to be fiscally and morally conservative.

Altogether, there are the proclamations of recent third party presidential candidates, and well-established political theory, to suggest that the two major political parties will fail to distinguish themselves in important ways. If so, the breadth of representation must be compromised. Yet others note counter-vailing evidence, or suggest that Democrats and Republicans are distinct in important ways. In the textbook noted above, the paragraph that follows the quote on major party similarities discusses the differences between Democrats and Republicans, stating, "These differences reflect differences in philosophy as well as differences in the core constituencies to which the parties seek to appeal."[12] To its credit, the textbook is presenting contrary academic points of view. In any event, we get arguments being made which suggest the two major political parties can be the same, yet different; a point that will be revisited straight ahead.

In recent years there has been an abundance of academic arguments made that suggest members of the two major parties will distinguish themselves in important ways, in part, because of the different social structures embedded in each.[13] Contrary to Downsian logic, researchers have found the positions of competing congressional candidates in marginal or competitive districts "diverge" from one another.[14] Beginning in the 1990s, in particular, it has been common for scholars to find evidence that the policy positions and voting behavior of legislators from the two major political parties are distinct.[15] For instance, it has been determined that party line voting in Congress has increased significantly in the past two decades. Party line voting is defined by first finding "party votes," or roll call votes in Congress where a majority of Democrats voted in opposition to a majority of Republicans. Once this subset of votes is determined, which removes from consideration unanimous or near unanimous votes on consensual and procedural matters, "party line" voting is a measure of how commonly Democrats and Republicans vote with one another on these party votes. This has been on the rise since the mid-1980s, suggesting major political party divergence and presumably an increase in the representativeness of the "big two" political parties.[16]

What should one make of these divergent arguments? Are the two major political parties not sufficiently distinct, yet very different? In large part, the answer is a function of the time period analyzed. In an earlier era, the two major political parties were more alike and consequently may have been less representative. Today, the big two are consistently more dissimilar in their policy preferences. What is unknown is the future. Will Democrats and Republicans continue to distinguish themselves in important ways in the next 20 to 30 years, or will we see a rebirth of cross-party voting and the lack of party discipline that defined Congress in the past?

The 20th century alone has seen several changes in the level of party distinctiveness. E.E. Schattschneider, in his classic work on democracy, notes that in 1912 the two major party campaign platforms were a lot alike.[17] During the New Deal of the 1930s, the two major parties differed more significantly on how to respond to economic crisis. Subsequently, in the 1940s and 1950s, cross-cutting cleavages and the institutionalization of the legislative process in Congress caused Schattschneider to bemoan the lack of party discipline and the failure of the two major parties to distinguish themselves in important ways.[18] Fast forward to the 1990s and party discipline and difference is alive again. This level of instability in the likelihood that the big two will consistently provide meaningful and representative electoral options does not provide a lot of confidence that the two major political parties will always represent a broad swath of society.

Yet something is missing from this discussion and the answer may lie in research published by the author of this book with his colleague Jeffery Mondak.[19] In that work, the policy positions of major party members in the House of Representatives were analyzed. Their issue positions were assembled from a survey conducted during the 1998 midterm election campaign. In short, the research found aggregate differences in the policy positions of House members from the two major political parties. More specifically, there were statistically significant differences in the stated policy positions of members from the two parties on 18 of 19 issues. The exception was the issue of Social Security reform where no difference was found. On issues as wide-ranging as abortion, gun control, taxes, and welfare reform there were statistically significant differences between House Democrats and House Republicans. But, there is a catch. The scales that were constructed for the purpose of testing partisan divergence ranged from 0.0 to 1.0 and in most cases Democrats and Republicans occupied positions in the center 50 percent of these scales. Thus, Democrats were typically about as far from the extreme left as they were from the Republicans and Republicans were equidistant from Democrats and the extreme right.[20] What was being represented was the middle ground. The research described the big two political parties as "center-left and center-right."[21] Positions such as "no abortion under any circumstance," "banning the manufacture and sale of new hand guns," and "tax increases to offset deficits and pay down the debt" were not, on average, being represented by either party. The implication was that representativeness was incomplete. Although Republicans were more likely to support abortion restrictions and Democrats were for more gun control, less than 5 percent of respondents, from either party, were willing to represent absolute positions on these issues.[22]

We can also look to polling data to get some sense of contemporaneous opinion on the subject of the representativeness of Democrats and Republicans, and by default, the representativeness of the two-party dominant party system in the United States. When asked, "How would you rate the job the Democratic/Republican Party is doing—offering solutions to the most important issues facing the nation?" in July 2010, 52 percent said the Democratic Party was doing either a "poor" or "very poor" job and 55 percent said the Republicans were doing either "poor" or "very poor." Only 8 percent felt either party was doing a "very good" job.[23] A different question asked, "How would you rate the job the Democratic/Republican Party is doing—putting the country's interest ahead of their own political interests?" Fifty-eight percent of the public felt the Democrats are doing either "poor" or "very poor" and 61 percent said the Republican Party was doing "poor" or "very poor." Again, roughly 8 percent of the people said the two parties were doing, "very good."[24]

The same poll measured party identification and found 42 percent of the respondents indicating they were either Republican or leaned toward the Republican Party, while 44 percent of respondents identified themselves as Democrats or leaning toward the Democratic Party.[25] Hence, over 80 percent of respondents were willing to classify themselves, in some way, with one of the two major political parties; but only 16 percent felt the parties were doing a very good job either addressing important issues or putting the country's interest ahead of their own. One can quibble with the manner in which this information is presented here. There are other ways to assemble and present this data. Yet the base story is one that has been told many times before.[26] A significant segment of the United States public is not captivated with the job either Democrats or Republicans are doing when they are given the chance to run the government.

Classic works on the determinants of quality democracy, by Austin Ranney[27] and E.E. Schattschneider,[28] point out the need for political parties to distinguish themselves in a "responsible" manner if democracy is going to be anything more than a façade. The basic argument is twofold. First, parties must take consistently distinct and meaningfully different policy positions. Second, they must vote accordingly. What seems to be happening in the United States, in the past two decades at least, is that politicians are reasonably responsible. Democrats and Republicans are more distinct and disciplined, but the breadth of their representative reach is questionable and surely does not encompass all points of view. It is also the case that one cannot, with confidence, predict that the two major parties will continue to be responsible. One does not know if, or when, the pendulum may swing back toward increased major party collusion in the future. In all, the distinctiveness of the two major political parties can be debated. The likely truth is they are distinct, but not overwhelmingly so. What is quite clear is that comfortable majorities of the public are less than perfectly satisfied with their electoral options.

Checking the Arguments Made in Support of a Two-Party Dominant Party System

People currently living in multi-party democracies may long for the simplicity of automatic majorities which comes with only two political parties in a national legislature. In multi-party systems, when no political party has a majority of seats, the party with the most seats is forced to find coalition partners whose support will help produce a governing majority. Once formed, the stability of coalition governments can be tenuous and this precarious quality can be discouraging. Government watchers may be concerned with the inefficiency that is a byproduct of instability. Still others may be concerned that minor political parties, which are part of a governing coalition, will be able to hold the policy-making process hostage, lest they obtain policy concessions. This may be especially frustrating if the minor party represents only a small fraction of the society. These arguments and their variants are the ones often used to support two-party dominance. What is missing, however, when people debate the pros and cons of a two-party dominant political system is careful consideration of all the different party system options.

Two-party dominance is commonly contrasted with a pure proportional representation system, with lots of political parties and coalition formation problems. Often there is limited consideration of alternative party system configurations. The late 19th and early 20th century United States experienced a political party structure that was different from what exists in the country today, but cannot be classified as a multi-party system either. There were two major political parties but third political parties were more electorally viable and more likely to influence policy agendas and outcomes. In addition, other Anglo-Saxon countries today use single-member districts and plurality rule election formats, have two dominant political parties, but also some third party success.

Political scientists have taken to calling these systems two-and-one-half party systems.[29] Under this scenario there are two major political parties that dominate and compete for majority party status. But, there are also third political parties that hold seats in the legislature and are given the opportunity to voice concerns and ideas. In some instances, the third party or parties can make a real difference when voting on specific legislative initiatives. Consequently, third parties are not the major players but they are not insignificant either. It is important to make this point because too often this option is not considered when proponents of the status quo in the United States make their case. The arguments commonly made by two-party advocates of the status quo in the United States are discussed in more detail below.[30]

The Separation of Powers May be Compromised

Some suggest that the United States system of separate elections for president and the legislature would be undermined by viable third parties. The argument goes something like this. A nation-wide election for the president forces political parties to be broad based. In multi-party systems political parties are more likely to have a local focus or be concerned with only a single issue. If the United States moved to a multi-party system, parties would have no incentive to be broad based and the current system, which has different constituencies electing the legislature and the president, would be compromised. The problem with this argument is that it has the causal direction mixed up. It might be the case that the separation of powers doctrine causes, or promotes, two-party dominance because parties are forced to be broad-based, but there is nothing to suggest that election laws will cause a governing system.

No reasonable argument can be made to suggest that the type of party system will cause a change in the separation of powers doctrine. A separate executive and legislative branch in the United States was "caused" by those who wrote the Constitution and nothing short of a constitutional amendment can cause this to be undone. The type of party system does not cause Constitutional arrangements. If there were a hundred political parties represented in Congress, nothing would change in terms of the president's veto powers, or the House of Representatives' ability to impeach executive or judicial branch officials. A separately elected president may force political parties to be broadly representative but small-successful political parties cannot cause a change in the separation of branches.

Geographic Representation would Suffer

The argument in this instance is that single-member districts cause effective geographic representation. By breaking a country or a state into legislative districts and allowing each district to choose a single representative, one is assured of considerable geographic representation. This is especially the case when one contrasts this to a pure proportional representation system, where the whole country, or maybe a whole state, is a single constituency. For example, if a whole state was one constituency, then all of the members of the legislature might hail from the northern half of the state and the southern half would go without representation.

The problem with this argument is that there are many ways to allow for viable third parties without getting rid of district elections. As we will learn, two-party dominance requires both single-member districts and a plurality rule. One could preserve single-member districts but use a majority rule and third parties would profit. Under a majority rule, if there is an election with three candidates and no candidate receives a majority of the votes cast there is a runoff between the top two vote getters. Let us assume the two major party candidates are the top two vote getters and the third party is not going to win. The third party, however, if their vote share is substantial can almost certainly influence who does win. This ability to swing the vote and affect the outcome of the race ought to encourage third parties to continue on from one election cycle to the next.

Moreover, it would be possible to preserve geographic representation and viable third parties with two-member districts. Two-member districts give third parties a chance because now they only need to be the second favorite political party in the district or constituency. Increasing the size of the national legislature would allow for two-member districts and very minimal change in other facets of the governing system.[31] A more complete discussion of this option will be discussed in the concluding chapter.

Party Primaries would Disappear

This argument, again, is most relevant when contrasting a two-party system with a pure proportional representation system. In many of the parliamentary-style democracies around the world that use proportional representation elections, political party leaders devise lists of candidates that they hope to seat in the national legislature. On Election Day people vote for a political party instead of a specific candidate and if their favorite political party receives 15 percent of the vote, the top 15 percent of the names on the party list gain seats. Representation is awarded in proportion to the level of public support. Allowing party leaders to choose candidates for public office is what concerns advocates of the status quo in the United States. This harks back to an earlier era in the United States, before party primaries, when political party bosses picked candidates. Many of these party leaders were allegedly corrupt, and the party primary system of selecting candidates was considered an important reform that helped to unravel the undue political influence of political party bosses.

The most glaring problem with this argument is that it assumes that the only alternative to two-party dominance is a party list system. The reforms discussed above, majority rule and two-member districts, would not require party lists and would be perfectly compatible with party primaries. Moreover, it is not clear that the party primary candidate selection process is perfectly desirable. Scholars note the tendency for party primaries to produce more extreme candidates because people who turn out to vote in primaries over-represent the more extreme elements of the party.[32] These same scholars note that party leaders may be more inclined to choose moderate candidates that would perform best in the general election.[33] Still more, arguments are made to suggest that the party primary system allows representatives of political parties holding public office to be less responsible and accountable. Since they are chosen in public party primaries, and not by party leaders, there is little incentive for these office holders to support or be accountable to their parties' positions on pending legislative matters.[34] Allowing party leaders to choose their candidates, on the other hand, takes the political party to task. Party leaders would have nowhere to hide; these are your candidates and their performance is your responsibility.

In all, it is not clear that the party primary candidate selection process is without fault. Even if one holds that party primaries are advantageous, there is no reason to believe that they could not exist alongside electoral options that promote third parties. Who knows, maybe someday a third party would be sufficiently successful to want to hold its own party primary nominating election. As it stands, third parties often have great difficulty finding a single candidate to run, let alone two for the same seat that would need to compete with one another in a third party primary.

Accountability would be Upset

Presidential-style democracy, with a separation of powers, causes significant accountability problems. If one political party controls the White House and the other political party the Congress, who is to blame when things go wrong? Defenders of a two-party system argue that the simplicity of a two-party dominant system aids accountability in a style of democratic governance that is already wrought with accountability problems. The United States uses a federal political arrangement, where power is shared between the national and state governments, again, making it difficult to place blame when problems arise. If one were to add multiple political parties, the accountability question would be further confounded.

This at first glance seems like a reasonable argument and one that sensibly supports maintaining the status quo party system in the United States. What this argument is missing, however, is a careful consideration of the relative accountability of the two political parties in the United States. Plurality rule elections and single-member districts create political parties that try to be all things to all people; they must capture the median voter's policy preference to win elections. Hence, the prevailing political parties water-down their message to make it seem reasonable to the most people, especially as the election draws near. In addition, public party primaries allow candidates to be disloyal to party leaders. Thus, there is very little in the way of accountability in a system with two catch-all political parties that do not empower their leaders with candidate selection.

Consider a system with more political parties representing more specific constituencies, with candidates chosen by the political party organizational leaders. One would know what each political party stands for and who to hold accountable. One would know which political party was truly pro-life, which was consistently for more states' rights, and which was willing to make the tough decisions to balance the national government budget. As it stands now, the two dominant political parties in the United States are very mixed in their performance in addressing these issues. An electoral system that allowed for viable third parties might produce candidates that could afford to take a stand on these issues. No longer would Democrats need to sound like Republicans, and vice-versa, as Election Day approached. People could be more confident when they placed their vote that their candidate, if elected, would represent their point of view. Accountability would be enhanced and not hindered.

Legislative Policy-Making would be further Deadlocked

Everyone recognizes that a system of government characterized by extensive checks-and-balances makes it difficult to pass new legislative initiatives. The Framers of the United States Constitution, clearly and unequivocally, desired to make it difficult for politicians to run roughshod over the citizenry by enacting new public policies easily. Supporters of two-party dominance argue that the automatic majorities inherent in a two-party system create opportunities to pass legislation that would not exist with multiple parties vying for attention and influence. An already difficult policy-making environment would be made more difficult with third party representation in the legislature.

A more complete response to this reasonable concern will be the subject of Chapter 4 in this volume. Suffice it to say, for now, that the historical record does not provide much evidence that time periods with no third party involvement have been significantly more productive than periods when third parties were more viable. The three most legislatively productive time periods in the 20th-century United States, without much debate, would be the Progressive Era, the New Deal Era, and the Great Society Era of the 1960s. In the first instance, a viable third party played a significant role in setting the legislative agenda that would ultimately pass and define this period as productive. In the second instance, a third party held many of the same policy prescriptions as the Roosevelt Democrats and voted with the Democrats to aid the passage of numerous landmark legislative acts. In the third instance, a rift in the majority Democratic Party between Northern liberals and Southern conservatives was instrumental in breaking the deadlock of the 1950s over Civil Rights and the problems of the inner city. The Intra-Democratic Party conflict broke the malaise of two-party collusion that was stifling legislative productivity mid-century.[35]

As it turns out, the checks-and-balances and the obstructionist tools available in the United States legislative process are sufficient that even when there are only two political parties, the minority party can prevent action. Historically, viable third parties, or factions within one of the major political parties, seem to have been able to prompt compromise and action. Both the theoretical arguments used to support this contention and empirical evidence intended to test the theory will be the focus of Chapter 4.

Election Margins would Decrease, Hurting the Legitimacy of Election Winners

The argument is made that with only two political parties contesting most elections the winner will always receive a significant percentage of the vote. This, in turn, provides legitimacy to the election winner that would not occur otherwise. But this argument fails on two accounts. First, under current rule, if third parties materialize, you still have the potential of a candidate winning the election with less than a majority of the vote. Presidents Lincoln, Clinton, and George W. Bush, to name a few, won the presidency with less than majority support and in each instance detractors used this to undermine their legitimacy. Second, a change to majority rule would ensure that the winner always had a majority of support and this would also promote viable third party electoral options.

Third Parties would get in the Way of Policy Moderation

The last argument made by two-party advocates, to be highlighted here, is that third parties representing ideologically extreme positions or single issues may hurt policy moderation, or even prompt radical change. The point missed by this argument is that the legislative process is defined by majority rule. A small third party in the national legislature would not be able to pass anything without major political party collaboration. If the intention is to value democracy and democratic processes, one must honor majority rule in the legislative process. In the case of the United States, because of checks-and-balances, super-majority rule is normally required and radical ideas face an even more daunting task.

If a third party, with radical ideas, became a majority party—their ideas could no longer be considered "radical." The same logic would apply if a third party was able to forge a working relationship with a major political party on a given piece of legislation. If third parties do not become the majority party or are not able to work with a larger political party, they will be marginalized. Assuming they hold truly radical issue positions, the democratic process will expose these to the public and this will compromise the third party's future electoral prospects. In today's Congress, good legislative ideas often never see the light of day. If policy prescriptions are indeed extreme, they almost certainly will not be brought before the national legislature. When they are, the process dilutes their intent.

Conclusion

In sum, many of the arguments made to support two-party dominance are incomplete. In part because two-party dominance is simply contrasted with a multi-party system and there is no consideration of party system alternatives. In other instances, the arguments made by two-party advocates simply do not jive with the historical record or other political realities. If one is willing to accept that there are reasonable alternatives to business-as-usual in the United States, it is necessary to move forward and attempt to understand how the status quo of two-party dominance was created. This is the objective of the next two chapters.

Chapter 2 examines a host of unique election laws to try and isolate the election rules and procedures that are responsible for third party failure. The 50 American states provide a nice testing ground because there is variation in the success of third parties and each state has distinctive election laws. Chapter 3 will look more closely at one particular election law that many third party advocates feel is particularly troubling. Democratic and Republican state legislators, over time, have found it convenient to pass laws that restrict third party ballot access. The disparities between major party and third party ballot access requirements have often been staggering. Fortunately, two states, Florida and Maryland, have rescinded their third party restrictions in recent years so it becomes possible to measure the effect these laws have had on overall third party success in those states. The conclusions will not be comforting to third party proponents.

Chapters 4 and 5 test the consequences of two-party dominance in the United States. First, Chapter 4 tests the effect of viable third parties on legislative productivity. In order to do so it is necessary to look back in time, to an era when there was more third party representation in the United States Congress to see if these parties made a difference. Did they spur legislative innovation or were they an anchor holding back legislative accomplishment? Before conducting this test, the chapter presents theoretical arguments about the structuring of party conflict that is most likely to produce policy innovation. Chapter 5 tests the relationship between viable third parties and citizen engagement. The bulk of the empirical testing will examine the association between the presence of third party candidates and voter turnout. The research, however, will also test for a relationship between third party prowess and civic engagement in the form of citizen-interest group density. The last chapter does more than provide a conclusion. Chapter 6 offers policy prescriptions and addresses what needs to happen to make viable third parties a reality in the United States.

Chapter 2

The Effect of Election Laws on Third Party Failure

As suggested in the last chapter, there have been many different election laws that have hampered third party electoral success. The primary culprits are single-member districts and a plurality rule. The former, denotes only one member, and only one political party, will represent each district or constituency. The later, suggests that one need not worry about pleasing a majority of the voters, just the most voters—or one more voter than the closest competitor. On the face of it these rules seem to make sense. One person represents one district and whoever gets the most votes wins. However, when one realizes there are other options that also make sense, such as requiring the winning candidate to receive a majority of the votes cast or political parties being represented in proportion to their level of electoral support, the election rules in the United States become more questionable. This chapter will begin by dissecting the two prevailing electoral arrangements discussed above to show how they promote two-party dominance and then test a series of other unique electoral arrangements to see what role each is playing in third party failure. Particular attention will need to be paid to the adoption of the Australian or "secret" ballot, because third party representation in the United States drops off significantly after this reform.[1]

Duverger's Law and Third Party Failure

Duverger's Law states that single-member districts and plurality rule elections create two-party dominant political systems. This postulate is widely charged with stifling the electoral prospects of third political parties in the United States.[2] There is a basic mathematical explanation reinforced by a psychological rationale for how and why this is the case. The mathematical explanation was alluded to in Chapter 1, and it has to do with the concept of a median voter. The median voter in any legislative district is the voter whose preferences lie in the middle. More specifically, there will be the same number of people in the district that are left of the median voter as there are people who are right of the median voter. Policy preferences can be multi-dimensional, so it is not quite this simple, but at least, in theory, there is someone with average or median preferences.

Figure 2.1 is intended to illustrate the mathematical explanation for Duverger's Law. If one were to plot the policy preferences of any constituency, the plot line would resemble a bell-shaped curve. There will be more people in the middle than there will be people who hold positions at either extreme. The median voter sets atop the plot line in Figure 2.1. When the election rule states that there will be only one person elected from each district, and whoever gets the most votes wins, political parties must scramble for the middle ground. It will not do much good for a political party to run on a platform representing extreme left or extreme right issue positions. That is not where the mass of voters lie.

Of course, it is common for people to claim there are some United States House districts that are more left-leaning and others more right-leaning, but this is irrelevant for the purposes of this illustration. The reason it does not relate is that a district leaning one way, or another, does so when compared to other districts or the country as a whole. The illustration represents a single district and in any single district there will always be more moderates than there will be people on the extremes. That is, more moderates in the district when compared to other people in that same district.

One can notice, in Figure 2.1, that there are only two sides to the position at the top of the curve. Because of the election rules used, only one person is getting elected to this district, and that one person has to simply corral the most votes. The latter suggests the need to moderate. Moreover, because there are only two sides to the median voter position, there is really only room for two political parties—one center-left and the other center-right. Thus, once Democrats and Republicans were established as a dominant political party they held a desirable position. They only needed to hug the middle to ensure their continued success. As noted earlier, Democrats try to sound like Republicans and Republicans try to sound like Democrats as Election Day draws near. This is purposeful: it is the key to their success in the general election.

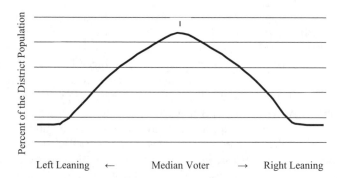

Figure 2.1 Duverger's Law and the median voter.

There is also a psychological rationale for why Duverger's Law holds up so well in the United States. The national legislature is quite small relative to the size of the population. There are only 435 positions in the House of Representatives and each voter gets only one member to represent them. Thus, very few people are interested in wasting their vote on a candidate that has little or no chance of winning. It may be that a voter's policy preferences are extreme left or extreme right, but it does not make sense for them to vote for a candidate or political party that represents these views if they are not likely to win. Better to cast a vote for the lesser of two evils or the dominant political party that is closer to your policy preferences. There are anecdotes galore that speak to this point. Did votes for Ralph Nader and the Green Party in 2000 cause the Democratic Party candidate Albert Gore to lose? What effect did votes for Ross Perot have on the electoral fortunes of Republicans in 1992 and 1996? The intention, here, is not to try to answer these questions. The point, simply put, is that too often votes for third party candidates are simply wasted. In other instances, they may cause your least favorite major party candidate to win. Hence, there is a considerable disincentive to vote for a third party candidate, even if their policy preferences are closest to your own.

Under current election rules there are both statistical and psychological explanations for why third parties fail. Yet one must understand that the same election rules exist in other countries today, countries where third parties enjoy some success. Indeed, these same election rules were largely in place in the United States during the second half of the 19th century when third parties did better at the polls than they do today. The implication is that there must be more to the story. What role, if any, is played by other election rules?

Other Election Rules and Third Party Failure

Figure 2.2 provides a timeline of the levels of non-major party representation in the United States House of Representatives since the mid-1850s, when the current two major political parties began their string of uninterrupted electoral supremacy. The vertical axis represents the percentage of House members in a particular Congress that were not members of the Democratic or Republican Parties. One can note that third party representation was quite common in the late 1850s and 1860s. During this time the two previously dominant political parties, Democrats and Whigs, had been factionalized. The party system was then disrupted by the ascendancy of the Republican Party, the last third party to displace an existing major party. The major party that lost out, of course, was the Whigs. Among the causes for the fall of the Whig Party was the inability of party leaders to reconcile themselves and their members on the issue of slavery, particularly slavery in new territories and states.[3]

But there is something else going on in Figure 2.2. Note, by the end of the 1890s, third party representation in the Lower Chamber of the people's branch of government was nearly non-existent and it was always less than

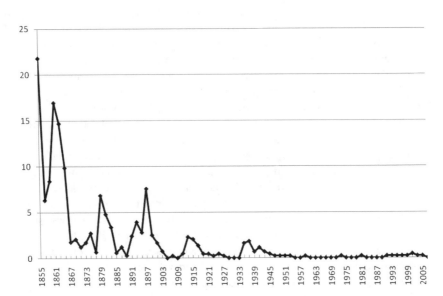

Figure 2.2 Percent third party representation in the House of Representatives, 1855–2005.

5 percent of the total membership. To explain this particular drop off in third party success, one must consider the role played by other election rules and in particular the adoption of the Australian ballot. The "secret" ballot meant political party leaders were no longer going to circulate ballots. Ballots would instead be produced by state legislatures. In some instances state legislatures transferred this power to county governments.

By the general election of 1892 the secret ballot had been adopted, in part, by all the American states at that time. The measure was instituted piecemeal in some instances and was not fully implemented throughout the country until 1950.[4] The purpose of the secret ballot was to temper the domineering tactics of political party organizations that would intimidate voters and whole communities into casting all their votes for the political party that held sway in that particular neighborhood, city, or region. But, the secret ballot had electoral consequences beyond the sequestered voting booth. It was no longer going to be the case that a third party could simply out circulate their ballot and beat back the major parties by force of effort. Instead, elected majorities in state or country legislatures would be charged with producing and disseminating ballots. These governing majorities nearly always represented one of the two dominant political parties. Thus, things got worse for third parties post-Australian ballot.[5]

Looking back at Figure 2.2, the two small upswings in the nearly flat line that occurs from the 1890s forward should be explained. Each comes about as the result of atypical circumstances, which temporarily advanced third party electoral fortunes. The first was the election of 1912, the last election where a third party presidential candidate, Teddy Roosevelt-Progressive Party, won more votes than a major party candidate. It seems the former president had coattails that helped to usher nine members of his new party into the House during the 1912 election cycle. Several of these individuals won subsequent re-election, which explains the carryover into the following four-year period. By 1917–18, however, major party dominance had reasserted itself and third parties fared poorly again. The second blip occurred during the Great Depression. There were eight members of the second Progressive Party, led by Robert La Follette (WI), and one member of the American Labor Party elected to the House of Representatives between 1935 and 1940. It seems severe economic hardship caused voters in some states to abandon the two major parties for a brief period of time. This is an important observation as it provides some rudimentary evidence that third party voting may serve as a channel for meaningful dissent, a topic which will be discussed in greater detail in Chapter 5.

One of the consequences of the secret ballot has been a drop off in third party success in American politics. What needs to be determined is what about the change has been, and continues to be, most damaging. As it turns out, the secret ballot engenders two significant changes in American electoral politics that need to be made perfectly clear. First, party leaders were prevented from circulating their straight-party line ballots. That is, third party and major political party officials could not simply circulate ballots with their candidates' names on them. This precluded the possibility of an ambitious third party candidate being able to out-hustle the major party competition. Second, the production and dispersion of ballots was granted to state government officials. A majority of these officials were either Democrats or Republicans who were now afforded the opportunity to erect institutional barriers in the form of ballot access laws and other restrictions for non-major party candidates to navigate.[6]

To date, the electoral barriers adopted in the wake of the secret ballot serve as the focal point for scholarly inquiry into the lack of third party voting and partisan independence in the United States.[7] Such impediments include a whole host of ballot access rules, the banning of fusion candidates, and closed political party primaries.[8] Ballot access restrictions include, but are not limited to, laws that require third party and independent candidates to collect a higher percentage of signatures than major party candidates in order to obtain a place on the ballot. Fusion practices, which allow candidates to run for office under multiple party labels, were banned. The practice of fusion candidacies benefits third political parties because they are able to nominate a candidate that runs under both their label and a major party label. In these instances, a voter can vote for this individual under either party label, which gives them the opportunity to show support for a third party without wasting their vote. Their vote is not wasted because the individual is also representing a major party with a realistic chance of winning. Party primaries are used to select candidates to run in a general election. Closed party primaries prevent voters who are not affiliated with one of the two major parties from participating in the candidate selection process. In effect, closed primaries force people into partisan corners so that they must join one of the two major parties or be shut out of the nomination process.[9]

Each of these barriers, just outlined, either singularly or in combination with one another, has been studied in some detail by those interested in the overall lack of third party representation in the United States. A preponderance of the third party research, however, has focused only on voting for presidential and gubernatorial candidates, choosing to explore how certain election rules work to promote major party dominance in elections to executive offices.[10] Breaking with this modal category of inquiry, this work assembles aggregate data on non-major party voting for United States House candidates—an area that has received less attention.[11] Using voting for elections to the House of Representatives provides a test of non-major party electoral competence in a showground where one might imagine minor party advocates would start a grassroots campaign for increased visibility and success.

The research reported in this chapter is conducted in much the same manner as other studies that explore the influence of auxiliary electoral barriers instituted by major party state government officials. However, the focus here is on the substantive effect of these changes and the possibility that preventing entrepreneurial third party leaders the opportunity to simply out-recruit their major party competition might be the real story. It must be stressed that the implementation of the secret ballot creates two new and independent electoral dynamics. We know it enabled Democrat and Republican state lawmakers to erect election barriers for third party candidates to navigate, but it also prevented the circulation of party-specific ballots. The former has been the subject of numerous studies—the latter consideration remains comparatively unexplored.

This chapter now moves to test the significance of three different election laws that have been written and adopted in some of the American states, post-Australian ballot—laws which, arguably, have contributed to third party failure in the United States. The three considerations are ballot access requirements, fusion candidate bans, and closed state party primaries. The 50 American states vary considerably in their contemporary adoption and use of these laws. Hence, the research takes advantage of the inter-state variation in election laws in the contemporary United States to test the substantive significance of the alleged third party barriers.

The Research Design

This test of third party failure covers the years 1976–2008. The start date represents the post-Watergate era. This is an appropriate starting point because

Congress changes as the result of Watergate. Specifically, there is a prolifera-
tion of subcommittees that decentralizes power structures and opens the door
for junior members to have more of a say in the legislative process. This, in
turn, conceivable creates a recruitment bias, or change in the types of people
who run for House seats.[12] The post-Watergate era marks the beginning of
what scholars have called the post-reform Congresses.[13] Moreover, extending
the test back in time runs the risk of mixing the modern electoral context
with earlier eras that did not witness the same basic political party allegiances.
For instance, prior to this time period the states that were dominated by
a single party were different. The "solid South," or the tendency for all
Southern states to elect only Democrats, began to deteriorate in the late 1970s
and particularly in the 1980s during the Ronald Reagan presidency. Given the
goal of this work is to learn the truth and consequences of two-party dominance today, the research does not mix earlier election eras with the modern
context.

The statistical models that follow will test the significance of the three electoral barriers to third party voting talked about above. Concerns over the
substantive significance of the relationships uncovered will be discussed in
the results section. That is, it will be necessary to know the size of the effect or
the magnitude of the relationship between the barrier and third party voting.
For example, one might find a statistically significant relationship between a
fusion ban and third party voting. Yet if third party voting in states with no
ban is only one or two percentage points higher than a state with a ban, this
obviously will not be enough of a difference to prompt third party electoral
success in most instances. The unit of analysis for the empirical tests is the
average level of non-major party voting in United States House elections
within each of the 50 American states. Fifty states and 17 election cycles
(1976–2008) yields a sample size of 850.

Figure 2.3 displays the average amount of non-major party voting in
elections for the United States House of Representatives, by year, from 1976
to 2008. Note, before 1990 non-major party voting nationwide was always
less than 2.5 percent of the total votes cast. With the 1990 midterm elections,
non-major party voting began to increase and reached a peak of nearly
6 percent of all votes cast in 1998. As we move into the 21st century, however,
non-major party voting begins to revert back to previous levels, and in the last
two election cycles reported (2006–08), non-major party voting hovers
around 3 percent.

The Dependent Variable: What the Research Seeks to Explain—Non-Major Party Voting

Non-major party voting is measured by the proportion of total votes cast in
United States House elections that went to third party candidates, independents, or write-ins from each state during each even-year election held in

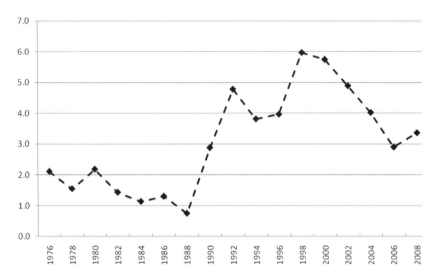

Figure 2.3 Percent non-major party voting in United States House elections.

November. Higher values denote the presence of greater non-major party voting in a particular state, during a given election year. Spoiled and scattered ballots are not counted as part of the total votes cast.

Figure 2.4 presents composite averages by state for the entire time period. Notably, Vermont exhibits the most extensive minor party voting during this time period. This is due to the successful political career of Bernard Sanders (I-VT), an independent member of the House of Representatives for 16 of the years included in the analysis. Vermont's 30-year average is just over 34 percent. The modeling that follows will take special precautions to account for the extraordinary success of Vermont's at-large, non-major party House member. Specifically, a dummy variable is created that equals "1" for the cases in the dataset where Bernard Sanders ran and won a House seat. This variable is found to be very highly significant as expected. More importantly perhaps, this finding suggests that non-major party success in the modern Congress is the result of unique individuals that run under peculiar circumstances. Sanders had served as mayor of Vermont's largest city for four terms and had considerable name recognition when he ran for a House seat.[14] In contrast to Vermont, the states of Georgia, Illinois, Maryland, South Dakota, Iowa, Florida, and North Carolina have the lowest third party voting—each averaging less than 1 percent non-major party support during the test period. The mean level of non-major party support, by state, for the time period is 3.10 percent, with a standard deviation of 7.09 percent.

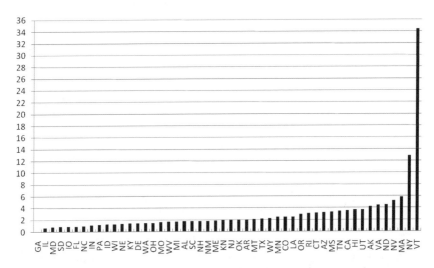

Figure 2.4 Percent non-major party voting in United States House elections, by state: 1976–2008.

Key Exploratory Variables—the Three Barriers

The first electoral barrier tested is restrictive ballot access laws or the ease with which candidates acquire a spot on an election instrument. The prerequisites for non-major party access (such as paying a monetary sum or acquiring a specific number of signatures) often exceed the requirements for major party candidates.[15] The presence of cumbersome filing fees and signature requirements, it is believed, reduces the likelihood non-major party candidates will run and depletes the resources of those who manage to gain ballot access.

Two measurements of the relative difficulty of ballot access are tested. In Model 1, Joshua Rosenkranz's interval-level ballot access scores are used.[16] His measure incorporates a host of ballot access considerations such as the number and the percentage of signatures required to gain ballot access, whether a filing fee is mandatory, and information about filing deadlines. Extended deadlines, with minimal fees, and fewer signatures are believed to facilitate ballot access. When ballot access laws have changed during the time period of this study, Rosenkranz's 1996 values are altered based on the formula he provides. The variable, in this study, ranges from 31 to 101 with higher scores indicating greater difficulty in ballot access for third party and independent candidates. The state with the least difficult ballot access during the time period of this study is Arkansas and the state with the most restrictive ballot access during this period is New Hampshire.[17]

In Model 2, Rosenkranz's ballot access index is replaced by a dummy variable scored "1" if the signature requirement for minor party candidates in the state exceeds 3 percent of a district's electorate and "0" if it does not. This simpler test represents a very strict ballot access requirement; only 6 of the 50 states had such a requirement for the entire time period of the study. In addition, the state of Florida had this requirement for part of the study period. On average, this straightforward and aggressive restriction ought to be associated with less non-major party voting. In both instances, the manner in which ballot access restrictions are calculated should produce negative associations with non-major party voting in the statistical models. Put differently, as ballot restrictions go up or grow in numerical value, there should be a corresponding decrease in non-major party voting, all else being equal.

The second consideration is whether or not fusion candidates are directly or indirectly banned in a state. Fusion allows two or more parties to endorse a single candidate. The candidate then proceeds to run under multiple party banners. Voters may opt to vote for a candidate under either the major party or third party label allowing them to send a message of approval to a third party and their candidate without "wasting" their vote.[18] When states place an outright ban on fusion candidacies, the viability of third parties is believed to be compromised.[19] Scholars believe the power of fusion candidacies to be so great for third party appeal that an addendum to Duverger's Law is offered: "Plurality election rules bring about and maintain two-party competition except where fusion candidacies are legally possible and other conditions, especially a competitive party environment, encourage their formation."[20]

In Model 1, fusion is operationalized by a dummy variable scored "1" if the state has placed a direct ban on fusion candidacies and "0" otherwise. Unfortunately, the exact quality of state laws regarding fusion candidacies is not always clear: many states neither ban fusion practices outright nor explicitly allow the practice. Hence, Model 2 scores this variable "1" if a state either directly bans or indirectly bans fusion candidates. In effect, this second measure includes all states that do not expressly allow fusion practices. Whether fusion is explicitly banned or ambiguously discouraged, a negative relationship with non-major party voting is expected in the statistical models.[21]

The third potential impediment to non-major party voting is the closed party primary. States with closed primaries require voters to register with one of the two major political parties as a precondition for participation in the party candidate selection process. Other states are more lenient and do not require major party registration to participate in primaries. Previous research suggests that closed primaries force voters into partisan corners[22] and produce less registered independents.[23] Voters who want to participate in a closed primary must join one of the two major parties. Hence, states with open primary election rules might be fertile ground for non-major party success.

It is important to note, however, that registering as an independent or a member of a third party is not the same thing as voting for a non-major party candidate in a general election. Previous research has suggested that there will be less people willing to register without party affiliation, or register with a third party, when primaries are closed. This is undoubtedly true, but this research is testing the factors that lead to actual third party voting in a general election. This is not the same as registering as a member of a third party prior to a primary election. In the general election, registered voters can choose to vote for whomever they like, without regard for party affiliation. One might imagine that if you are forced to join a major party, this affiliation may carry over to the general election and cause less non-major party voting, but this is not necessarily so.

To illustrate, consider protest-minded voters in a state with an open primary. These individuals may be satisfied by their opportunity to vote strategically in the major party primary. For instance, voting for a candidate they like but do not believe can win. They might then make a more sober choice in the general election, choosing the major party candidate they view as the least of two evils. In contrast, independent-minded voters in a closed primary state might be alienated by their state's "closed" system and consequently cast a protest vote in the general election. If this were the case, it might be difficult to find a statistical or substantive relationship between the type of primary and non-major party voting. In the empirical test, a state's primary system is considered closed and scored "1," when a state requires major party registration prior to voting in a party primary. All other primary types that exist in the American states are coded "0."[24] Consistent with the literature on party registration, the expectation is that closed primaries will result in less third party voting, however, because of the argument just elaborated, expectations are not strong.

Key Control Variables

It is not enough to simply test for correlations between the electoral barriers outlined above and non-major party voting. It is important to control for other factors that might also influence third party fortunes. For instance, it may be the case that states with tough ballot access laws are also states with one dominant major party. If it were also the case that states with a dominant major party are less likely to vote for non-major party candidates, one might find a relationship between ballot access and non-major party voting that is spurious. That is, the correlation between ballot access restrictions and non-major party voting may be caused by a third consideration, "one-party dominance." Hence, it is important to control for other possible explanations when testing the independent influence of election laws on third party success. Multiple regression analysis allows one to test the relationship between variables while holding the other considerations constant.

The first key control variable is a measure of the proportion of House elections in each state that went uncontested by a major party candidate in each election cycle. If there are many instances in a state where either Democrats or

Republicans are left off the ballot, this might prove fruitful for non-major party candidates. If it is true that nature abhors a vacuum, third party voting should rise as a reaction to the presence of ballots with only one major party candidate.[25] Specifically, this variable is measured by calculating the percentage of House races in a state, in a given year, which did not have both major parties contesting the seat. For instance, if a state has been apportioned four seats in the House of Representatives and one of them went uncontested by a major party candidate, the variable would equal ".25." If none went uncontested the variable would equal "0.0." If all four seats were uncontested by one, or the other major political party, the variable equals "1.0," and so forth. A positive coefficient, or association with non-major party voting, is anticipated.

Second, the percentage of self-identified independents in each state is accounted for. One might imagine states where citizens are more inclined to identify themselves as "independent" ought to have more third party voting. Data from 1985 research on state citizen ideology are employed in the models as an estimate of self-identified independents.[26] Again, a positive coefficient is anticipated.

Other Control Variables

Four additional control variables are included in the models. First, the research will test for more non-major party voting in presidential election years. Many recognize that there have been some marginally successful, and visible, third party presidential candidates during the time period of this study—John Anderson and Ross Perot to name two. In the case of Perot, he is on the ballot in all 50 states for two different election cycles. The expectation is that the presence of third party presidential candidates might prompt more non-major party voting down the ballot. Put differently, third party presidential candidates might have "coattails" that will prompt more non-major party voting in races for the House of Representatives. Of the 17 election cycles included in the analysis, nine of them are presidential elections and those cases are all scored "1," the others are scored "0." A positive association between this variable and third party voting is anticipated. That is, there ought to be more non-major party voting in House races in presidential election years.

Second, the degree of one-party dominance present in each state is considered.[27] As alluded to, one might expect that if voters in a particular House district or state are extraordinarily loyal to one major party over another, they might also be less likely to support non-major party candidates. One-party dominance is measured as the absolute value of the difference between the percent of each state's lower chamber that is from the Democratic Party and the percent that is from the Republican Party.[28] For example, if a state House is split 50/50—half Democrats and half Republicans—the variable would equal "0" suggesting no "one-party dominance." This produces a scale that theoretically could range from 0 to 100, where higher values denote a state

House dominated by one major political party. The research is expecting a negative association. If one party dominates the state legislature, the variable will take on higher values and this ought to be associated with less non-major party voting, all else being equal.

Third, the ideological distance between a state government and its citizenry is accounted for. Given that the major parties control state governments, throughout the country, one can imagine that if governing officials do not represent their constituents ideologically, this would be a potential boon for non-major party candidates. It is believed a greater ideological distance between elected officials and those they represent will be associated with more non-major party voting. In effect, the third party vote serves as a protest against the major political parties.[29] The variable is measured using the absolute value of the distance between composite scores of state government and state citizen ideology developed by previous research.[30] Unique values are available for each state in two-year increments and a positive association with non-major party voting is anticipated.

Finally, the research uses a simple dichotomous variable to control for the electoral success of Bernard Sanders (VT). The eight cases in the dataset representing an instance where Sanders wins Vermont's at-large House seat are scored "1" and all other cases are scored "0." As alluded to earlier, this test will certainly return a strong positive and statistically significant relationship with non-major party voting. The Appendix to this chapter describes the particular statistical model that is used to accomplish the testing.

Results

When Rosenkranz's interval level measure of ballot access is employed (Model 1 in Table 2.1) a statistically insignificant relationship is found between ballot access restrictions and non-major party electoral success. This is likely troubling for third party advocates because so much ink has been used to suggest that equal ballot access was a major explanation of third party failure in the United States. When the ease of ballot access index is replaced with a simple dichotomous variable capturing whether or not the signature requirement for ballot access is greater than 3 percent of the district electorate, the variable does achieve statistical significance. The coefficient (which can be viewed under the heading "Model 2" in Table 2.1), however, is not substantively promising. Eradicating this particular barrier is associated with less than a 2 percent increase in non-major party voting, on average.

There were seven states that, at some point during the time period studied, had this type of stringent ballot access requirement. The results of this test suggests that if these states were to reduce this requirement to something more manageable for third parties we might expect third parties to gain about an additional 2 percent of the vote share, on average. Unfortunately, a 2 percent average improvement in vote share would only in very rare instances increase actual

Table 2.1 Testing the Effects of State Election Laws on Non-Major Party Voting for U.S. House Seats, 1976–2008

Model: Random-Effects Tobit[a]

Independent Variables

	Exp. Sign	Model 1: Coefficient (standard error)	Model 2: Coefficient (standard error)
Election Laws			
Ease of Ballot Access Index	+	.00 (.00)	
More than 3% Sig. Required	–		−2.00* (1.03)
Fusion Directly Banned	–	−1.69* (.84)	
Fusion Indirectly Banned	+		−1.50* (.84)
Closed Primaries	–	.88ᵗ (.66)	.71 (.64)
Key Controls			
Major Party Missing	+	8.59*** (1.23)	8.41***
% Self-Identified Independents	+	.11** (.05)	.11** (.04)
Other Considerations			
3rd Party Presidential Candidate on Ballot	+	.58ᵗ (.39)	.58ᵗ (.39)
One-party Dominance	–	−2.83** (1.13)	−2.78** (1.11)
Citizen/Govt. Ideological Distance	+	.04* (.02)	.04* (.02)
Vermont	+	27.88*** (2.46)	27.91*** (2.42)
Constant		−3.76* (2.22)	−5.13** (1.80)
Chi²		271.78***	281.44***
n (17 election cycles × 50 states)		850	850

Notes
*** $p < .001$; ** $p < .01$; * $p < .05$; ᵗ $p < .10$ (one-tailed tests)
a The coefficients represent the marginal effects of the independent variables on the dependent variable, with the condition that the data are uncensored or that the dependent variable is greater than zero. See the Appendix for more details on the statistical model used.

independent candidate or third party representation. Moreover, because there is nearly no non-major party representation in the House from any state other than Vermont, during the time period of the study, one cannot reasonably suggest that this barrier has been preventing independent representation.

Fusion bans in both models are statistically significant. Whether fusion candidacies are explicitly or indirectly banned, the non-major party vote share is reduced. However, the reduction in vote share, again, is not substantively promising for third party activists: less than 2 percent, on average. Scholars have argued that fusion candidacies represent the best chance for third parties to obtain some reasonable amount of success.[31] Under the existing single-member district and plurality rule formula this may be true. However, an average increase in vote share of less than 2 percent does not strike one as particularly promising. Moreover, besides Bernie Sanders (I-VT), there has not been a non-major party member in Congress from one of the ten states that currently allow fusion candidates since Thomas Alford held a seat from Arkansas as an Independent in the 86th House (1959–60).[32]

The third perceived barrier, the closed state party primary, as it turns out is not associated with any noticeable change in the non-major party vote share. This was *not* entirely unexpected. Barbara Norrander argues that closed primaries will produce fewer independents, but not necessarily more partisan behavior.[33] It seems forced partisanship tends to be shallow.[34] It may be that some individuals, prone to be independent and wishing to cast a protest vote, are satisfied by their ability to vote strategically in an open primary and subsequently opt for a major party vote in the general election. There is no increase in the vote share for non-major party candidates associated with party primaries that are closed—or open for that matter.

The control variables seem to be telling the real story. Each of the six tests, representing control variables, return coefficients in the hypothesized direction and five of the six variables are easily statistically significant in both model runs reported in Table 2.1. The coefficients for major party missing (Models 1 and 2) suggest that there is about an 8 percent increase in non-major party voting when comparing a state that always has a major party missing with a state that never does. The percentage of self-identified independents in a state is associated with greater non-major party voting in both model runs as well. A 1 percentage point increase in self-identified independents is associated with a little over a one-tenth percentage point increase in non-major party voting, on average. Consistent with expectations, one-party dominant states are associated with lower levels of non-major party voting and a greater ideological distance between a state government and its citizenry is linked to more minor party voting. Finally, non-major party voting in Vermont when Bernard Sanders is running is more than 27 percentage points higher, on average, all else being equal.

In the end, the results suggest that eliminating the three alleged electoral impediments does not hold much promise for increasing third party representation in the United States Congress. The test is specific to the United States House, but the strength of the findings provides considerable confidence that the results are applicable to the legislature more generally defined. Indeed, evidence from this research suggests that one of the considerations, the closed party primary system, does not hinder non-major party success at all. Stringent ballot access requirements, and the direct and indirect banning of fusion candidacies, are both statistically linked to less non-major party voting, but the substantive gain for non-major party candidates is not promising. Moreover, there is no relationship between these laws and more actual non-major party representation in the House of Representatives. Instead, when the occasional non-major party candidate has emerged in American politics, they have been helped by other factors such as name recognition and campaign resources.[35] The conclusion drawn by this analysis is that meaningful reform, directed at dismantling the partisan duopoly, in the United States must come from changes in the higher-order electoral barriers, specifically, the single-member district and plurality rule arrangements.

It was indicated earlier that there was some third party success in the United States prior to the Australian ballot, which allowed election system barriers to be erected that frustrated third party organizations and their potential supporters. The lack of any substantive significance associated with these barriers, in this research, suggests the other accompanying change associated with the secret ballot is responsible for stifling non-major party success; namely, the eradication of party ballots which prevented minor parties from simply out recruiting their major party opponents. Learning this, however, does not point immediately to a solution. If the barriers were found to be more significant, their elimination would be the answer. Since the auxiliary barriers are not responsible for the lack of third party representation a solution is more elusive.

Getting rid of the secret ballot and returning to party-produced ballots is not plausible. Altering or abolishing single-member districts or plurality rule together likewise would be a daunting task. It is important to remember, however, that it requires both features—both single-member districts and plurality rule elections are necessary for Duverger's Law to hold. Changing either one of the two holds promise. The concluding chapter to this book will discuss this in more detail, as well as another possible solution to the lack of third party electoral success in the United States.

Conclusion

In the 50 years before the Australian ballot was put into play, non-major party candidates held, on average, more than 5.5 percent of all seats in the United States House of Representatives. Arguably this level of representation would be normatively appealing today, given historically that many quality policy proposals (including Progressive Era reforms such as the direct election of senators and women's suffrage) were advocated for in third party platforms. Previous research has implied that the electoral barriers created when major party governing officials took control of ballot construction and dissemination must be the answer to the drop-off in non-major party success in the

20th century and today. Researchers have found statistically significant relationships between these barriers and third party voting and concluded they were correct. Yet a closer examination shows that regardless of how these alleged impediments are measured, the substantive significance of their influence is minor. Thus, eliminating these barriers is not likely to revive third party electoral success and representation. This research has suggested that there must be more to the story.

The advent of the Australian ballot engendered two crucial changes. First, the reform allowed major party state legislators to pass laws restricting non-major parties. Second, it prevented non-major party leaders from being able to circulate electoral instruments with their candidates' names on them. The second change now appears the most consequential. The real story has been the inability of entrepreneurial minor party leaders to out-hustle their competition. In sum, this is the change that broke the back of third parties in the United States.

Joseph Cooper, an important congressional historian, writes about electoral competition for House seats—pre-Australian ballot:

> state and local parties dominated the electoral system. Nominations for local, state, and national offices were all determined by party caucuses or conventions. The parties [major and minor] also controlled the conduct of election campaigns. In these campaigns the primary strategy remained the mobilization of partisans through reliance on parades, stump speeches, party workers, and party newspapers. Similarly, the parties controlled the machinery of elections. Voting eligibility remained in the hands of partisan election judges at the polls—present day registration laws did not exist. Ballots continued to be printed by the parties, confined to party candidates, distinctively colored, and handed in the open to these same judges at the polls.[36]

The scenario described by Cooper no longer exists. Many would suggest that it is entirely appropriate that political parties are not as powerful as they once were. But, with reform came the inability of minor parties to simply out recruit and outwork their major party brethren. This research finds that elimination of the lower-order electoral barriers, such as ballot access restrictions, fusion bans, and closed party primaries, cannot bring about a meaningful increase in third party representation.

There will nevertheless be many third party advocates who will want to believe that if they only had equal ballot access, they could compete. Statistically significant relationships encourage them. The belief that ballot access is the major problem is so widespread, among third party proponents, that this research will devote another chapter to testing the effect of ballot access laws on third party electoral fortunes. The states of Florida and Maryland have removed ballot access restrictions for third parties in recent years and it is possible to test specifically what difference this is making in these states. Upon completion of this analysis it is hoped that we will know the truth about two-party dominance and can then turn to its consequences.

Appendix: Model Specification

A major issue with model specification in this research is that the dependent variable is left-censored. The percentage voting cannot go below 0 percent and for 107 of the 850 observations the dependent variable equals "0." This is problematic for Ordinary Least Squares regression, which assumes that values on the dependent variable are continuous and can take on any value. Moreover, the percentage of voters, who would have supported a non-major party candidate, if one had appeared on the ballot, is unknown. Simply creating a dichotomous control dummy variable for those cases where the dependent variable equals "0" is not ideal. This approach will underestimate the intercept and overestimate the slope, potentially producing inconsistent or biased esti-mates.[37] Consequently, this study employs a Tobit model that accounts for the censoring. Tobit produces consistent estimates of the parameters when the data are censored.[38] Tobit coefficients can be interpreted similar to Ordinary Least Squares regression coefficients with the exception that the coefficients represent the marginal effect of the independent variables on the dependent variable, with the condition that the data are uncensored or that the depen-dent variable is greater than zero.

A second issue with the statistical test reported here is that data on the dependent variable are arrayed both over time (election cycles from 1976–2008) and across sections (the 50 American states). This suggests the need for a random-effects specification, which provides estimates that are weighted to correct for heteroscedasticity and autocorrelation problems that occur in many pooled/cross-sectional research designs.[39] Hence, a random-effects Tobit model is used. The model is run in Stata 9 using the command "xttobit." The random-effects Tobit model uses an adaptive Gauss–Hermite quadrature to approximate the high-dimension integrals that are part of the likelihood for these models. Quadrature is one of the most accepted approaches to fitting these models.[40] A quadrature check was performed with varying integration points that produced consistent estimates, indicating that the data are stable and the model is correctly fitted. Results of these tests are available from the author upon request.

Chapter 3

More of the Truth

Ballot Access Reform in Maryland and Florida

The results of research reported in the previous chapter suggested that an excessive signature requirement is linked in a statistical manner with less third party voting in the American states. The magnitude of the effect, however, was not promising for third party advocates. It was also learned that Duverger's Law, which holds that single-member districts and plurality rule elections create two-party dominant political systems, is the best explanation for the stifled electoral promise of third political parties in the United States. And the drop off in third party success, post-secret ballot, has more to do with the inability of third parties to outwork their major party brethren than it does any election system barrier created by state government officials. The former finding, regarding Duverger's Law, may be new to many who do not study political parties. Yet, it is routinely acknowledged by scholars who study party systems, with some noting exceptions to the "law."[1] The latter finding, which suggests that ballot access may not be the real issue, will be met with skepticism by many political party scholars. Many will want to continue to argue that facilitating more egalitarian ballot access is likely the most meaningful source of reform for third party promoters.[2] Part of the reason this argument is made, undoubtedly, is that reformers see change in other aspects of the electoral system as unrealistic. Many will hold out hope that the removal of ballot access restrictions will mean more third party success.

Most frequently, suggestions for easier ballot access prescribe lowering the number of signatures required to gain a place on the ballot or alternatively allowing a candidate to simply pay a fee to gain ballot access.[3] To examine the topic of ballot access more completely, this research takes advantage of election rule changes that occurred in the state of Florida in 1998 and the state of Maryland in 2003, which explicitly removed the major party advantage in obtaining ballot access. In the first instance, the change came about as the result of a state constitutional amendment which received broad support from Florida voters, and in Maryland the change came via legal wrangling in the state court system. Specifically, the research looks for evidence of increased third party contestation rates, increased third party voting, and third party election wins, post-reform. Actual electoral victories will be the best evidence that these rules really make a difference.

This chapter begins by elaborating how the rules were changed in Florida and Maryland. This is particularly important for third party activists who might seek other changes in election rules to facilitate third party success. It should be clear that the Florida and Maryland experiences represent real change to election laws and that those who might claim change is never possible are wrong. Third parties gain equal ballot access in both states in a bona fide manner. Next, looking at each state's experience separately, empirical evidence is presented to test the questions outlined above. Does the removal of third party ballot access restrictions increase third party contestation rates, voting, and electoral success? The first tests simply compare third party contestation rates and third party voting pre- and post-reform. A difference of means test will be conducted to ascertain if there is statistically significant change in any of these considerations. Then, the research uses each Florida and Maryland House District as a unit of analysis and looks for factors that influence the level of third party voting. For example, the amount of competition between the two major political parties varies by District in both states. This analysis will be able to test the influence that major party competition has on third party voting irrespective of the nature of ballot access laws. The intention is to employ a more fully specified statistical model to try to isolate what is most affecting third party voting, beyond the ballot access arrangement.

Ballot Access in Florida

After the presidential election of 1928, Florida legislators were allegedly embarrassed that 2 percent of the state's voters had supported the Communist Party candidate for president.[4] The state therefore instituted a policy of third party exclusion by erecting ballot access barriers, such as significant signature requirements and prohibitive filing deadlines. Between 1928 and the constitutional change that took place in 1998 there were numerous legal challenges to Florida's ballot access rules; but state and national courts regularly rejected the charge that they were discriminatory.[5] Moreover, in the 20 years leading up to 1998, legislation to ease ballot access requirements were introduced in the state legislature and rejected eight times.[6] Until the twilight of the 20th century, the state of Florida "remained hostile toward candidates outside the Republican or Democratic parties."[7]

In 1997, the Florida Constitution Revision Committee (CRC) was meeting to hear proposals from interest groups and the general public for changes to the state Constitution. In Florida, a CRC is appointed by the elected leadership of the state and the state's chief justice every 20 years and is charged with prescribing possible changes to the state Constitution. At public hearings, in 1997, restrictive ballot access laws were lamented with regularity.[8] More specifically, the CRC was lobbied by a coalition of third party interests united under the banner of Floridians for Fair Elections,[9] which argued "that it's easier to get on the ballot in St. Petersburg, Russia as an independent than it is in St. Petersburg, Florida."[10]

Libertarian Party activists, in particular, mobilized supporters to call for change at every hearing held before the CRC in 12 cities across the state during the summer of 1997. Eventually members of the Reform Party, Green Party, Natural Law Party, and Socialist USA Party, in addition to advocates from Common Cause (a group that presses for "better and cleaner" elections), would attend the hearings.[11] This ideologically diverse coalition lobbied in unison for ballot access change. The proposed solution, Revision 11, was the first-ever proposed amendment to the state Constitution to receive unanimous approval by the CRC for placement before the voters.[12] The committee vote was 28–0, with nine committee members absent.[13] The ballot measure, subsequently, was approved by state voters in the 1998 midterm election, with 64 percent of the voters supporting the change.[14]

Specifically, Revision 11 held that ballot access for non-major party candidates could not be more difficult than it is for the party with the largest number of registered voters in a given district or constituency. Prior to Revision 11, ballot access laws in Florida were often unique to individual counties but always very prohibitive for third parties. For example, most counties had a rule that the two major political parties could obtain ballot access by collecting signatures from 3 percent of their party's registered voters or by paying a fee. In contrast, non-major party candidates were made to collect signatures from 3 percent of all registered voters in the relevant constituency and had no option of paying a fee.[15] Once passed, the wording of the Revision allowed for two possible legislative interpretations. The legislature could respond to Revision 11 by making ballot access for the two major parties more difficult, changing nothing for third parties, or it could make third party ballot access easier.[16] They opted for the latter and additional ballot access restrictions for third parties were removed, state-wide.

In order to test the effects of removing all ballot restrictions for third parties in Florida, data are collected by United States House district for nine election cycles, including the four elections that took place prior to Revision 11 (1992–98) and the five subsequent elections (2000–08). The nine election cycles represent 215 observations. During the first ten years of the time period studied, Florida had 23 House districts and during the last eight years it had 25 House districts. The decision was made not to extend the analysis back any further than 1992 because the state witnessed a fundamental shift in major party allegiance in the late 1980s; namely, the legislature switched from being predominantly Democrat to predominantly Republican. During this period of major party disruption one might expect anomalous third party support, although a review of vote totals suggest that this did not happen. In any event, by 1992, this major party realignment had settled in a considerable manner and consequently the test looks at third party success in this new major party alignment period.[17]

Ballot Access in Maryland

The state of Maryland had always had relatively restrictive ballot access laws, but was able to make things worse for third parties in 1971. Beginning that year, Maryland required third parties to overcome a two-tiered ballot access restriction. First, non-major parties had to qualify as a "valid" party. To do so the party had to collect signatures from 10,000 registered voters and the petition signatures would be scrutinized by the Maryland Board of Elections. In addition to the 10,000 signatures, however, each individual third-party candidate was also required to conduct a separate petition drive and obtain valid signatures from 1 percent of the registered voters in the jurisdiction they wished to represent, creating a two-tiered hurdle. A candidate running for governor, for example, would have had to collect approximately 30,000 additional signatures, after his party collected the initial 10,000 signatures.[18]

As the result of Maryland's ballot access restrictions, third party candidates in the state were scarce during the last quarter of the 20th century and there was some public dissension. In 1996 the Maryland Senate failed to pass a bill, passed by the state House, which would have reduced the number of initial signatures required for third party validation or recognition.[19] By 1998, however, a new bill circulated in the state legislature and passed, which successfully lowered the number of initial signatures required to validate a third party. The new law went into effect in 1999 but this was only a small improvement and the state remained one of the very few states in the country that maintained some type of two-tiered ballot access requirement/restriction. Even after the law changed in 1998, only eight states had more aggressive restrictions than Maryland in terms of total signatures required for third party ballot access.[20]

Under these stringent ballot access requirements the Maryland Green Party was established in 1990 after successfully submitting a petition with more than 10,000 signatures. The legal challenge to Maryland's laws, however, did not occur until the 2000 election cycle when Green Party nominee David Gross chose to run for a seat in the United States House of Representatives in an attempt to represent Maryland's fifth congressional district. According to Maryland's two-tiered requirements, Gross was required to submit a petition signed by at least 1 percent of the total number of registered voters in the district. Gross successfully submitted the petition but the state election board invalidated over one thousand of the signatures because they represented "inactive" voters. These were legally registered voters, but voters who did not vote frequently. As a result, Gross was not qualified. The Green Party sued the state election board, arguing that several of Maryland's ballot access restrictions were unconstitutional (*Maryland Green Party, et al. v. Maryland Board of Elections, et al. 2003*).

The case advanced to the Court of Appeals, the highest court in Maryland. There, the Court ruled in favor of the Maryland Green Party, stating that various regulations passed by the legislature and implemented by the Maryland Board of Elections violated Article 1 of the Maryland State Constitution. The legal matter centered on the actions of the Maryland State Board of Elections. The Court argued it was not constitutional to invalidate voters, simply because they failed to vote frequently. Then, the Court went even further, ruling that the two-tiered petition requirement, for third parties in Maryland, was discriminatory and a violation of the equal protection component of Article 24 in the Maryland Declaration of Rights. The ruling pointed out that the two major political parties in the state (Democrats and Republicans) were able to use support in previous elections as justification of their legal status and that a candidate who decided to run as an independent, without party affiliation, was also able to circumvent the two-tiered requirement. Hence, the two-tiered requirement was arbitrary and capricious.

The Maryland Board of Elections appealed the Court's ruling in an attempt to preserve the restrictive ballot access laws. The matter remained tied up in the legal system until 2003 when the appeal failed and the matter was settled, once and for all, in favor of third parties. Since 2003, the second-tier ballot access restriction for third party candidates in Maryland has been removed and recognized third parties have been able to freely nominate candidates for the general election ballot. The question becomes, did the removal of the ballot access barrier increase third party electoral competition and third party electoral success in Maryland post-2003? In the empirical testing that follows, the time period 1996 through 2008 will be examined: four election cycles prior to the removal of third party restrictions and the three election cycles since their removal. In the case of both Maryland and Florida, an attempt is made to examine roughly the same number of district elections before and after the ballot access change occurred. In the case of Maryland, there are only three election cycles since the change has been fully in place therefore those elections are compared to the previous four election cycles.

The Research Design

The empirical analysis begins by illustrating the actual number of United States House races that were contested by non-major party candidates in the two American states pre- and post-reform. This is followed by a comparison of non-major party voting in each state during the two time periods. Finally, output from a multiple regression analysis is presented, for each state, which controls for other possible explanations for non-major party voting. Special attention will be paid to the substantive significance of any change in the vote share that is associated with the ballot access reforms.

The Dependent Variables: What the Research Seeks to Explain—Non-Major Party Contestation, and Voting

The first test for change looks to find higher levels of non-major party contestation, post-reform. The level of non-major party contestation is calculated by simply counting the number of elections that had someone other than a Democrat or a Republican receiving a vote during the time period before the reform and the time period after the reform. The second test is for vote change or the level of votes received by non-major party candidates, on average. Again, the test will be to compare the earlier time period with the post-reform period. When examining vote shares, the proportion of votes received by all non-major party candidates in each United States House district is used. Even more specifically, the total votes cast for all non-major party candidates in each House district is divided by the total number of votes cast for all candidates running in the district. In addition to third party votes, this calculation includes votes for candidates who ran without a party affiliation as well as write-in candidates.[21]

The non-major party vote shares, pre- and post-reform, are first examined alone. Then the values become the dependent variable in the regression analyses. Specifically, the non-major party vote total in each district during each election cycle becomes the unit of analysis. In Florida, the sample size will be 215. In Maryland, during the time period examined there are always eight United States House districts and seven election cycles are analyzed, so consequently the sample size will be 56.

The largest percentage of votes for non-major party candidates, in Florida, occurred in a 2006 election when two candidates running without a political party affiliation garnered a combined total of 31 percent of the vote in District 12. These candidates, however, were easily defeated by the Republican candidate in the race. In Maryland, the most non-major party voting also occurred in 2006. In this instance a Green Party candidate running for the District 5 United States House seat received over 17 percent of the vote and write-in candidates received 0.8 percent of the vote. Notably, the election in Florida took place without a Democrat on the ballot and the election in Maryland took place without a Republican on the ballot, which points to an important potential explanation for non-major party success: a major party missing from the ballot.

The Key Exploratory Variable—Ballot Access Reform

The key explanatory variable is the change in ballot access laws that took place in each state. In Florida, the post-reform era begins with the 2000 election and in Maryland the 2004 election cycle. In each instance a simple dichotomous variable is employed. Elections prior to the reform are scored "0" and those following the reform are scored "1." In the regression analyses, a positive association is expected between the non-major party vote share and the removal of ballot restrictions. A substantively significant coefficient, one of considerable magnitude, will indicate the importance of ballot access restrictions to third party success, vis-à-vis Duverger's Law.

Control Variables

In the regression analyses there are four control variables employed. First, the models account for whether a major party, Democrat or Republican, is missing from the ballot. Predictably, non-major party voting will be higher when one of the major parties is missing. The variable is scored "1" if a major party candidate is left off the ballot and "0" otherwise.

Second, district party registration statistics are considered. In particular, the research controls for the percentage of a district's electorate that is not registered with either of the two major parties. Florida's and Maryland's election divisions provide values by United States House district for each of the election cycles in the analyses. This type of data is not available in all states and that is why in Chapter 2 the decision was made to use the percentage of self-identified independents. Intuitively, a positive association should manifest between the percentage of voters without a major party affiliation and non-major party success. It should be noted, however, that there are important conceptual distinctions between registering with a third party or opting to remain non-affiliated and actually voting for non-major party candidates in a general election. The latter is evidence of behavioral independence, whereby action is actually taken in support of third parties, and the former requires only attitudinal independence or a willingness to consider oneself "independent."[22]

Third, the models control for whether there was a third party presidential candidate on the ballot when voters were considering whether to support third party candidates for the United States House. Presumably, a third party presidential candidate might have "coattails" that sweep-in some support for third party candidates further down the ballot. In each of the two states in each presidential election year, during the time period of this study, there were multiple third party presidential candidates on the ballot. Therefore, a dichotomous variable is created, scored "1" for each case that took place in a presidential election year and scored "0" in congressional midterm elections and a positive association with third party voting is anticipated.

Finally, the models control for one-party dominance. Recall this was found to be significantly associated with non-major party voting in Chapter 2. In the previous chapter, the research used the absolute value of the difference in major party representation in the lower chamber of the 50 state legislatures as a surrogate for one-party dominance. Since the analyses here are specific to a single state, this measure will not suffice. Instead, one-party dominance is measured as the level of electoral competition between Democrats and Republicans in each House district, in each election cycle during the time period studied. Particularly, the absolute value of the difference between votes cast for Democrats and Republicans is calculated. A larger number will indicate more one-party dominance in the district, a factor believed to hurt third parties. If a district's citizens are consistently supporting one of the two major political parties, one might imagine that this level of "one-party dominance" is not fertile ground for non-major party voting. Conversely, if the district elections are close, this may indicate a district culture that embraces electoral competition and voters may be more open to voting for a third party challenger. As the value of this variable grows, non-major party voting is hypothesized to go down; hence, a negative coefficient is anticipated.

Results

Figures 3.1 and 3.2 display the non-major party contestation rates in Florida and Maryland respectively. In Florida, the elections that occurred during the period prior to the implementation of Revision 11 (1992–98) were contested by non-major party candidates only 39 percent of the time. After the reform, the average contestation rate rose to 56 percent. In Maryland, 72 percent of United States House races were contested prior to 2003 and the 24 House races that have occurred subsequent to the change in ballot access have all been contested by non-major party candidates. The increases in both states are statistically significant at the 95 percent confidence level.

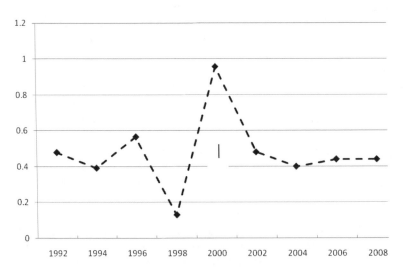

Figure 3.1 Percent non-major party contestation rate: Florida U.S. House races[a].

Notes
| Denotes the change in ballot access laws.
a Dif. of means test for two time periods (1992–98 and 2000–08); $t = -2.12$ ($p < .05$, two-tailed test); $n = 215$.

Source: Florida Secretary of State-Division of Elections

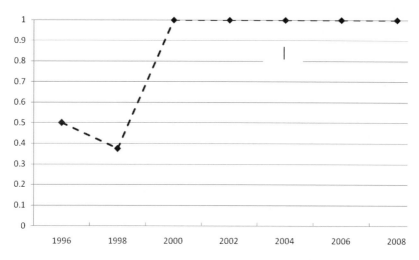

Figure 3.2 Percent non-major party contestation rate: Maryland U.S. House races[a].

Notes
| Denotes the change in ballot access laws.
a Dif. of means test for two time periods (1996–2002 and 2004–08); $t = -3.09$ ($p < .01$, two-tailed test); $n = 56$.

Source: Maryland State Board of Elections

A closer inspection of the figures, however, reveals some curious results. Examining Figure 3.1 one can note that the 2000 election, in Florida, the first following the passage of Revision 11, is driving the apparent boon in non-major party contestation rates. Indeed, if this election is removed from the mix, the statistically significant increase in the level of contestation disappears ($t = -.68$). Thus, it seems that non-major party candidates did initially take advantage of easier ballot access. However, in succeeding elections they retreated to pre-Revision 11 contestation levels—perhaps in light of the fact that easier ballot access did not translate into election victories. In Maryland, Figure 3.2, one must take note that the increase in third part contestation rates actually occurred in the 2000 election cycle, and was maintained in the 2002 election cycle, before the Court finally removed the second tier ballot access barriers in 2003. One might imagine that the minor reduction in the first tier restriction that took place in 1998 caused non-major party enthusiasm and higher levels of contestation. Nonetheless, it is not the case that contestation rates changed markedly immediately pre- and post- the 2003 change.

Next, the research considers actual votes cast for non-major party candidates. Figures 3.3 and 3.4 exhibit the mean vote percentage garnered by non-major party candidates in each of the elections studied. In Florida, Figure 3.3, the difference of means test for the two time periods, pre- and post-reform,

Figure 3.3 Percent non-major party vote share: Florida U.S. House races[a].

Notes
| Denotes the change in ballot access laws.
a Difference of means test for two periods (1992–98) and 2000–08); $t = 2.06$ ($p < .05$, two-tailed test); $n = 215$.

Source: Florida Secretary of State-Division of Elections

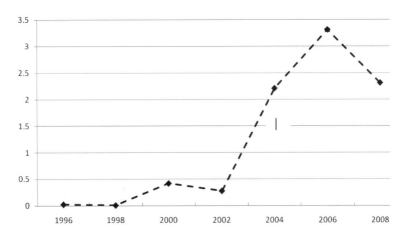

Figure 3.4 Percent non-major party vote share: Maryland U.S. House races[a].

Notes
| Denotes the change in ballot access laws.
a Difference of means test for two time periods (1996–2002 and 2004–08); $t = 4.04$ ($p < .01$, two-tailed test); $n = 56$.

Source: Maryland State Board of Elections

shows the expected increase in the non-major party vote share (t = 2.06, p <.05 two-tailed test). Consistent with the issue of contestation, however, it seems that the election directly following the change, 2000, was the most consequential. In contrast to the analysis of contestation rates, however, when the 2000 election is excluded from the analysis, a marginally significant increase in the non-major party vote share does remain (t = 1.79, p <.10 two-tailed test). The value for 2008 holds particular promise for non-major party advocates in Florida, representing the highest total since 2000.

Another interesting observation from Figure 3.3 is the mean non-major party vote total for the 1992 election cycle in Florida. The roughly 2 percent support for non-major party House candidates is atypical for the time period. It may be that the sensational presidential bid of the independent candidate Ross Perot increased voters' enthusiasm for choices beyond the major parties.[23] If so, this suggests the importance of controlling for presidential election years, when non-major party candidates routinely appear on the ballot to contest for the nation's highest office.

In Maryland there is also a marked increase in non-major party voting post-2003. Unlike contestation rates, which increased prior to the removal of the second tier ballot access barrier, non-major party success increases in a significant manner only after the 2003 Court decision. The difference of means test for the two time periods is easily statistically significant (t = 4.04, p <.01 two-tailed test). But one cannot help but look at the vertical y-axis to learn more about the substantive significance of this change. The 2006 election cycle, in Maryland, brought in the highest percentage of non-major party voting, but the mean total did not even reach 3.5 percent of all votes cast in United States House elections that year. A 3 percent increase could be consequential if third parties were already receiving considerable support but a 3 percent increase from nearly no support, prior to the reform, is not going to make much of a practical difference.

Table 3.1 presents the results of the regression analyses. Column one displays the results from Florida. Note, straight away, that the ballot access change is statistically significantly associated with more non-major party voting. The Tobit coefficient for this variable can be interpreted in a manner similar to the more common Ordinary Least Squares coefficients.[24] Specifically, the coefficient value of 3.97 suggests nearly a 4 percent increase in non-major party voting in Florida, after holding constant the other considerations in the Model. This seems promising, but again the increase represents an increase in support over practically non-existent support so it is difficult to get too excited. In contrast, one should note the coefficient derived from the test of "Major Party Missing." This variable, in Florida, is associated with more than a 15 percent increase in non-major party voting, a rationally more promising consideration.

The second column presents the results from Maryland. Here ballot access change is, again, statistically significant. The results suggest that one can be over 99 percent confident that there has been an increase in non-major party

Table 3.1 Non-Major Party Voting by U.S. House District: Florida 1992–2008 and Maryland 1996–2008

Model: Random-Effects Tobit[a]

Variables	Exp. Sign	Florida: Coefficient (standard error)	Maryland: Coefficient (standard error)
Ballot Access Change	+	3.97** (1.57)	2.02*** (.56)
Major Party Missing	+	15.29*** (2.98)	8.84*** (1.55)
% of Registered Voters w/out Major Party Affiliation	+	.20ᵗ (.15)	.07ᵗ (.05)
3rd Party Presidential Candidate on Ballot	+	3.34** (1.05)	.66 (.55)
Lack of DEM/GOP Electoral Competition (one-party dominance)	–	–.18*** (.04)	–.12 (.15)
Constant		.54 (2.14)	–1.43 (1.35)
Chi²		40.66***	68.90***
n		215	56

Notes

*** *p* < .001; ** *p* < .01; * *p* < .05; **t** *p* < .10 (one-tailed tests)

a The coefficients represent the marginal effects of the independent variables on the dependent variable, with the condition that the data are uncensored or that the dependent variable is greater than zero. See the Appendix to Chapter 2 for more details on the statistical model used.

voting in Maryland since 2003. The coefficient derived from the test, however, suggests only about a 2 percent increase. On the other hand, when a major party is missing from the ballot in Maryland, non-major party voting is nearly 9 percent higher. In all, the smaller sample size and fewer election cycles post-reform, in Maryland, need to be considered. Conceivably, more data representing additional election cycles will spur better results; but for now, the practical significance of the increase in non-major party support cannot be considered reassuring for third party advocates. Ballot access restrictions alone do not seem to be a sufficient explanation for third party failure.

Considering the other variables in the models, "Major Party Missing" is statistically significant in both Models. Arguably, the best chance for third party candidates, given current election rules, is to try to fill the competition vacuum created by the absence of a major party. Districts where the percentage of registered voters who are not affiliated with a major party is higher are associated weakly with more non-major party voting. The confidence level has to drop to 90 percent to claim a statistically significant relationship in both Florida and Maryland. This somewhat weak relationship had been anticipated, as previous research notes this possibility.[25] In particular, Marjorie Randon Hershey, an authority on political parties in the United States, suggests it is much easier to be an "attitudinal" independent than it is to be a "behavioral" independent.[26] People may not want to align themselves with either of the two major parties, but these same people are not necessarily loyal to non-major party candidates in a general election; perhaps, in part, because they do not wish to "waste" their vote.

Presidential election years, in Florida, are associated with a little more than a 3 percent higher non-major party voting, although this consideration is not significant in Maryland. The level of major party competition, a surrogate for one-party dominance, is statistically linked to less non-major party voting in Florida. The test for Maryland returns a negative coefficient, as expected, but it is not statistically significant. In all, the smaller sample size in Maryland compromises the test of these variables. Although it is not safe to assume that stronger relationships would necessarily be revealed if there were more data.

Conclusion

The Democratic and Republican office holders, in Florida and Maryland, either explicitly or implicitly supported legal barriers to the inclusion of third parties in electoral competition for many years. Once the ballot access barriers were removed, the threat of a non-major party candidate winning elections to Congress from these states became, in theory, more realistic. That is, a charismatic third party candidate could conceivably captivate the electorate of a Florida or Maryland House district and win a seat in the national legislature. Yet this has not happened. No third party or independent candidates have won United States House seats in Florida or Maryland since reform took place. It is important to note that no non-major party candidate has won a seat in either of the state legislatures as well.

Moreover, findings from this research suggest, at best, non-major party candidates have increased their vote share by about 4 percent. Therefore, the research presented in this chapter provides further evidence that the single-member district plurality rule hurdle is simply too difficult for third parties to transcend. Ultimately it appears that Duverger's Law and not ballot access is what moderates or prevents non-major party electoral success. As a way to illustrate this finding, one can turn briefly to consider another state that *did not* follow the single-member district, plurality rule election prescription for a period of time. It is difficult to test the effects of this base electoral format on third party fortunes in the United States because there is so little variation in the use of this election arrangement.

However, from 1872 to 1980, the state of Illinois elected members to the state House of Representatives in three member districts by way of cumulative voting.[27] The rules allowed voters three votes to distribute among up to three candidates, usually out of four. This voting method was designed with the

Table 3.2 Non-Major Party Representation: Illinois State House (1872–2006)

Time Period	Total # Legislative Seats	Total Seats Held by Non-Major Party	% Non-Major Party Representation
Multi-Member Districts (1872–1980)	8727	138	1.58
Single-Member Districts (1982–2006)	1534	0	0.00

Source: Michael J. Dubin, Party Affiliations in the State Legislatures: A Year by Year Summary, 1796–2006 (Jefferson, NC: McFarland and Company), 2007.

explicit aim of enhancing third party representation. Table 3.2 compares the proportion of state legislative seats held by representatives of minor parties in Illinois during the period of multi-member districts and the subsequent period of single-member districts. During the period of multi-member districts, the state averaged about 1.5 percent minor party representation in the state legislature. Since the adoption of single-member districts there has been no non-major party representation.[28]

In sum, the Australian ballot reform allowed major party state legislators to pass laws restricting non-major party ballot access. It has been widely held that this allowance, in part, is responsible for the overall lack of third party representation in American legislatures. The evidence from Florida and Maryland is that this may not be so. Although there is some additional electoral support for non-major party candidates associated with the removal of ballot access restrictions, there is nothing close to the level of support needed to prompt actual electoral victory. Moreover, in the state of Florida in particular, the increase in levels of contestation and non-major party voting appear to be more a product of the novelty of equal ballot access than anything like a sustained grassroots effort to establish new viable third political parties.

Chapter 4

Third Parties and Landmark Policy Productivity

This chapter starts from the premise that the capacity of a legislature to produce landmark acts depends significantly on the character and regulation of conflict within the institution. Substantial and sustained landmark productivity requires a legislative workplace that fosters real policy contestation characterized by serious conflict, so that difficult policy problems can be brought to its attention. But the legislature must then maintain internal conflict within moderate parameters to avoid institutional meltdown and enable deliberative policy-making to proceed. Seen in this manner, legislatures experience a polarity paradox, with too little as well as too much conflict hindering landmark productivity. The enactment of landmark laws comes amidst moderate conflict.[1] Although this thesis is intended to speak to the legislative process in democracies, generally, the theoretical discussion and empirical test that follows will focus on the United States Congress.

If the premise outlined above is allowed and one wants to tie third political parties to legislative productivity in Congress, then third parties must help moderate conflict. Third parties must be capable of intensifying discord when major party conflict is too low and attenuating dissension when it is too high. Put differently, under conditions of legislative malaise third parties would need to be able to stir the pot or stoke legislative debate. On the other hand, when the two major parties have ramped up partisan rhetoric and passion, third parties would need to be a calming influence cooling partisan warfare and refreshing the legislative agenda. In order to test this thesis empirically, case studies of third parties who have gained representation in the United States Congress in the late 19th and early 20th century will be conducted. First, however, it is important to provide a more complete discussion of the hypothesized relationships. Specifically, one has to appreciate the argument regarding the importance of moderate conflict to legislative productivity and also come to recognize how third parties might be expected to accomplish this.

Why Third Party Representation Might Prompt Legislative Productivity

The Democratic and Republican parties have not only varied in their levels of inter-party disagreement over time but also their intra-party homogeneity. In many respects these are related concepts. Given two political parties, if one party is heterogeneous in its policy preferences, this might easily result in overlap with the opposition party, reducing inter-party conflict. On the other hand, if parties are internally homogeneous this might prevent similarity between the two parties and inter-party distinctiveness and conflict would be more prevalent. In distinguishing the level and character of conflict that exists between the two major political parties, scholars have taken to analyzing what is commonly referred to as party polarization, or major political party distinctiveness in voting behavior. Polarization may result from more intra-party homogeneity, more inter-party difference, or both.[2]

The level of major party polarization is seen as a central factor shaping the intensity of conflict in Congress and the logic of politics that dominates policy-making in a legislature.[3] As Congress moves from low inter-party polarization to high inter-party polarization, it moves from a context in which intra-party differences dominate policy-making, amidst substantial inter-party similarities, to a context in which inter-party differences dominate policy-making, amidst substantial intra-party similarities. Party polarization can thus be seen as a continuum from low to high, as in Figure 4.1. The center of that continuum represents a realm of moderate polarization. As one moves from left to right, intra-party differences are normally declining while inter-party differences are increasing.

This research is suggesting the middle of the polarization spectrum, as exhibited in Figure 4.1, provides the best opportunity for policy productivity. Furthermore, as a conflict scenario in Congress moves away from the middle, it is possible to imagine "T" points, or tipping points, where the focus of partisan conflict shifts in a manner that creates problems for substantial and sustained legislative productivity. To the left of the first T in Figure 4.1 the level of inter-party differences is dwarfed by intra-party differences and one

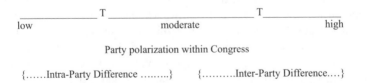

Figure 4.1 Major party polarization and the differentiation between intra-party difference and inter-party difference as the dominant conflict scenario.

Note: Moving away from the center, the "T"s designate critical tipping points at which the dominant style of policy conflict, either intra-party difference or inter-party difference, moves to a level believed to compromise policy productivity.

might imagine the power of party leaders will be compromised because of dissension within their ranks. To the right side of the second tipping point, inter-party differences will be pronounced and there may be little common ground from which two-party negotiations might be expected to take place.

When thinking about the relationship between third political parties and landmark policy-making, it is helpful to differentiate the character of conflict that exists between the two major political parties in the manner just described. Specifically, intra-party difference and its accompanied lack of inter-party distinctiveness suggest the possibility that there will not be sufficient structuring of conflict to create meaningful policy options. Third political parties, in this instance, might appear as mavericks or outsiders with little stake in the status quo of inactivity. Their stranger status might allow them to stimulate meaningful policy debate and prompt a consequential legislative agenda. Alternatively, intense inter-party conflict between the major parties often spurs elaborate and sophisticated use of obstructionist tactics by the minority party to prevent majority rule and productivity.[4] In this instance, third parties might serve as moderators, members who are divorced from the passion of intense inter-major party rivalry, a rational voice each major party might seek to hear as they attempt to forge allegiances or simply escape the drama of intense inter-party contestation.

The theoretical underpinnings of these arguments beg further elaboration. The arguments being offered about aggregate levels of major party conflict and policy productivity are most relevant if the party system is two-party dominant. A two dominant political party legislative arrangement creates relatively straightforward arguments about the role of partisan conflict in the legislative process. For instance, under conditions of two-party dominance and a depolarized legislative process there is a simple yet critical problem for generating landmark productivity. Because of heightened intra-party differences and negligible inter-party discord, minimal conflict will exist over public policy between the two major parties, while substantial policy conflict will exist within each party. In such a situation no clear and opposing tilt exists to partisan division over policy on behalf of which the articulation of distinct party policy positions might occur. Such a scenario may have an underlying disquiet, but nonetheless is unproductive because it is too easy to simply ignore problems because there is no loyal opposition to hold the process accountable.

Yet there is a second problem for productivity in a depolarized setting. In the face of intra-party conflicts over policy rank-and-file, party members will be hesitant to give party leaders procedural and organizational power that might be used to identify, construct, and pursue a partisan agenda, lest these powers be used to pressure members to support policy positions against their personal commitments and electoral interests. Thus, while the parties might be close enough in ideological and policy terms to compromise and enact landmark legislation, and close enough in size that neither can presume to enact policies on their own without compromise, they have no policies to debate owing to inter-party agreement, intra-party conflicts, and leaders without the authority to construct differential policy agendas, negotiate compromise, and push the enactment of legislation.

The mid-20th-century United States Congress was depolarized in the manner just described. Conservative Southern Democrats often agreed with minority Republicans on foreign policy issues. Liberal Democrats and Republicans both supported civil rights for minorities in opposition to conservative Southern Democrats. Western and Northeastern Republicans often differed on trade and monetary policies, while each had their allies in the Democratic Party. During many of these years, the speaker of the House of Representatives and/or Minority Leader Sam Rayburn (D-TX) directed new members of Congress with the maxim "to get along, go along," and there were no third parties in Congress that might disrupt the status quo that bordered on collusion when senior Southern Democrat standing committee chairs were content to work with Republicans to protect the status quo of inactivity on matters of civil rights, health care reform, environmental degradation, a plethora of inner-city issues, and rural poverty.

With so many cross-cutting major party cleavages, an overall lack of major party discipline, and ineffective structuring of policy options it is not surprising that President Harry Truman's Fair Deal did not produce major legislative accomplishment. Or, that equal rights for minorities and women were left on the legislative back burner during the 1950s. As we move into the decade of the 1960s, extraordinary circumstances surrounding political assassinations, combined with increasing levels of party polarization, move major party distinctiveness into the moderate realm resulting in Congress becoming productive for a time. President Lyndon Johnson's legislative accomplishments are well known, but there was also success in the administration of President Richard Nixon in dealing with major environmental problems, via successful clean air (1970) and clean water (1972) legislation.[5]

If one follows this story line into the 1980s, and then into the 21st century, the description changes from one of moderate party polarization to one of hyper-major party polarization. The two political parties become consistently distinct and Congress experiences a period of obstructionism. Because landmark legislative accomplishment is most-often based on a retrospective judgment, it is difficult to judge "productivity" in a contemporary period.[6] However, once one controls for presidential honeymoons, shocks to the political system in the form of terrorist threats, and financial crisis, it is reasonably safe to assume that the modern era has not been extra-ordinarily productive.

The intention of the discussion of policy productivity in the post-World War II era is to show how moderate levels of conflict might be more productive. The account does not involve third political parties because the period just described did not witness any reasonable level of third party electoral success. Simply put, the 1960s and early 1970s witnessed a moderate level of partisan conflict[7] and the period has been judged more productive based on different measurement techniques.[8] Because there were no third political parties in Congress, it is safe to assume that third parties are not a necessary condition to prompt moderate conflict. In the empirical tests that follow, it will be important to determine whether third parties, in an earlier era, were a sufficient condition to prompt conflict moderation and ultimately landmark legislative productivity.

Putting aside the theoretical argument about how depolarization, weak leaders, and insufficient structuring of legislative conflict can produce legislative stalemate, it is important to note the polarized spectrum also confronts problems when it comes to producing landmark achievement. As Congresses approach the extreme right-hand side of the spectrum (see Figure 4.1 for a visual), maximum policy differences will exist between the two major parties while great policy agreement will exist within each of the major parties. In such a situation, a clear and opposing tilt exists between the major parties so they will have many policy differences to articulate and contest. Each party's members are sufficiently cohesive in their agreement on policies that they may be willing to give their leaders great procedural and organizational powers to pursue these differential policies.[9] In principle, a united majority would seem able to vote down a united minority and enact its legislative agenda.

But, even in a single chamber of Congress there are multiple stages to the policy-making process and each stage, most commonly, requires majority support. The need for concurrent majorities, mathematically, determines the need for a supermajority level of approval. Moreover, procedures in Congress can be so complex that a united minority can easily obstruct the majority in meaningful ways. This induces the need for inter-party compromise and negotiation on procedural issues and even on policy content. Obstructionism is magnified by bicameralism and in particular Senate rules, which require a supermajority for policy enactment. In the 21st century, the Senate still honors the norm of unlimited debate or filibuster and three-fifths of the entire Senate, currently 60 votes, is required to kill a minority party hold on legislation. Under conditions of hyper-major party polarization, defined by strict two-party discipline, and no cross-party commitments, the legislative process will shut down. Majority parties are simply not large enough to get their way.

But there is a second problem for productivity under conditions of high polarization or hyper-conflict in a democratic legislative system. Homogeneous political parties often mean more ideological extreme party members. These members may have been elected in bitter partisan elections; having come out victorious, members may assume they have a mandate for their ideological agenda. These individuals, when confronted with the need to compromise in order to enact policies, may oppose doing so because they promised constituents to deliver on a precise partisan agenda. Moreover, because the majority party's leaders will have been given great powers to deliver on the party's agenda, they will not want to water down the party program lest they dilute their support. For their part, minority party members may oppose compromise in anticipation that a great defeat of the majority party on critical policy issues may mobilize the minority's base and aid capture of the Congress in the next election cycle. To those who have followed closely the workings of the recent Congresses this storyline should resonate well.

Thus, while the parties operating in a Congress at the extreme right end of the polarization continuum may be far enough apart to articulate distinct policy agendas and cohesive enough to give their leaders significant powers with which to pursue a partisan agenda, the complex realities of congressional politics may impose on them a need to compromise that is likely to be thwarted by rank-and-file members of the two major political parties. Given this scenario, the enactment of landmark legislation becomes difficult as majority party members are too sure of themselves to be willing to compromise and minority legislators see majority party legislative accomplishment as a stumbling block to their future electoral success.

In sum, when attempting to tie viable third political parties to legislative achievement, it is important to understand something about major party legislative conflict. In particular, it is important to recognize the paradoxical role played by major political party polarization. Within the depolarized spectrum, when a decrease in conflict inhibits landmark productivity, third party involvement may increase conflict and inject a level of interpersonal conflict between members sufficient to break loose agenda items, increase the saliency of a relevant agenda, and awaken the citizenry to the "do-nothing" major parties. An energized legislative environment and a more informed public may in turn facilitate productivity.

Within the polarized spectrum, where conflict between the major parties is the threat to innovative policy-making, third party members will likely not be the primary target of partisan attacks, will not be a part of major party power struggles, and almost certainly will not have the same animosity toward either of the major parties as they will have toward one another. Moreover, third parties may be in a position to calm the legislative environment because members are likely to have a unique view of the significant policy puzzles confronting society, which can be elaborated in committee meetings and on the floor of the legislative chambers. Given a polarized legislative environment, viable third parties might help members of the big two political parties interact with a mutual regard that aids negotiation and compromise.

Given the expectation that third parties ought to be able to moderate legislative conflict and previous research that suggests moderate conflict is most conducive to landmark legislative productivity,[10] it seems prudent to move forward by carefully looking for empirical evidence to either confirm or reject this thesis. Anytime an attempt is made to test a particular theory, measurement assumptions must be made that will need to be scrutinized. Specifically, in the research design offered below it will be necessary to discuss and cautiously choose a measure of meaningful third party involvement in the legislative process, and to prudently establish a measure of landmark legislative accomplishment. In the end, this judicious approach is necessary in order to test whether third party involvement causes legislative accomplishment.

The Research Design

It can be noted in the test of third party involvement in legislative productivity, the research does not settle for a simple relationship between the existence of third parties in Congress and the sheer quantity of legislative activity. Instead, the test will be to see if a relationship exists between publically recorded third party agendas and the passing of new laws. Moreover, the new laws will need to be designated "landmark" by the method describe below.

Testing the theory that third party involvement in the legislative process can moderate extreme conflict and ratchet up conflict when major party collusion and/or malaise have crept in is not a straightforward proposition. Among the primary concerns, already noted, is the level of third party involvement sufficient to produce these effects. But, also important, is the lag between some minimal level of third party success and results in the form of legislative productivity. Not to mention the problem of defining meaningful productivity.

There has been considerable academic effort to produce statistical models capable of illuminating legislative gridlock and/or productivity.[11] At issue in many of these well-intentioned efforts is the inconsistency in the results. For instance, it is still not clear what effect divided government plays on legislative accomplishment. Some argue that it makes little difference theoretically,[12] or empirically,[13] while others argue that unified government is more productive,[14] while still others suggest it depends on the configuration of conflict in the legislature in the time period being considered.[15]

Rather than produce yet another statistical test of variables that may determine legislative productivity in an era of third party success when data is sparse, this research will use a case study approach. Specifically, third parties that reach a minimum level of representation in Congress during the current two-party dominant era will be studied to determine whether the issues they concern themselves with were ultimately addressed by Congress. But even more specifically, if the issues with which they concerned themselves resulted in laws that retrospective judgment has deemed laws of "landmark" proportions.

Measuring Third Party Involvement in Congress

The process for measuring viable third parties in Congress was initiated by first determining a minimum level of third party electoral success to study. Although it is possible that the mere presence of third parties in electoral contests might influence the legislative process,[16] it seems more reasonable to study some minimal level of actual third party representation in Congress. The theory espoused above suggests the causal mechanism by which third parties might affect landmark productivity has to do with their position as antagonists or facilitators in the actual legislative process. Hence, this research will look to test third party involvement when third parties are actually present in the national legislature.

Assuming there is a certain level of membership in Congress which would be necessary for third parties to influence the legislative process is one thing; determining precisely what minimal level of representation is sufficient is conspicuously unknown. One can safely exclude the modern era, which has witnessed no third party representation. Moreover, it makes sense to limit the analysis to the post-Civil War era to hold constant the two major political parties that third parties would be commingling with in Congress. This has the added benefit of analyzing a time period defined by the same two dominant political parties that exist today.

The analysis begins with the Liberal Republican Party, which gained notoriety in American politics in the 1870s, opting not to include a variety of third parties that existed in Congress in the immediate aftermath of the Civil War that had the word "union" in their name. These parties often were simply a cover for Democrats and Republicans that were trying to take advantage of nationalism and patriotism in the war's aftermath. Beginning with the 43rd Congress (1873–75), the analysis continues through the 76th Congress (1939–40) when third parties all but disappear from the United States Congress.

Next, the decision is made to exclude from the analysis political parties that managed to seat only a single member in either the House of Representatives or Senate. But also, because the House of Representatives is considerably larger than the Senate, the decision is made to require a higher threshold for the lower chamber. Hence, this study focuses only on third parties that were able to place at least three members in the House of Representatives and/or at least two members in the Senate in the time period defined above. The notion is that third parties who have reached one of the minimal thresholds of representation in one or the other chamber will be third parties that might be expected to make a difference. Table 4.1 exhibits the third parties that will be considered, by chamber, by the relevant Congresses, and by their level of representation.[17]

Considering Table 4.1, one can notice there are a total of eight third parties with the level of representation in Congress just specified. Of these, three of the parties, the Nationals, the Roosevelt Progressives, and the La Follette Progressives never saw representation in the Senate. On the other hand, one of the eight third parties, the Silver Party, never gained representation in the House of Representatives. Four other political parties managed to gain representation in both chambers. All else being equal, one might expect those gaining representation in both chambers to be more successful. In particular, the Populist Party was able to manage a minimal presence in both chambers of Congress for an extended period of time: through the 1890s and into the 20th century. A second third party that needs to be considered carefully is the Roosevelt Progressives. Although the Party never achieved representation in

Table 4.1 Multi-Member Third Party Representation—Congress, 1872–1944

House of Representatives

Third Party	Congress (Years)	# of Members
Liberal Republicans	43rd (1873–75)	4
Nationals-Greenbacks	46th (1879–81)	13
Nationals-Greenbacks	47th (1881–83)	10
Re-Adjusters	48th (1883–85)	4
Populists	52nd (1891–93)	8
Populists	53rd (1893–95)	11
Populists	54th (1895–97)	9
Populists	55th (1897–99)	22
Silver Republicans	55th (1897–99)	3
Populists	56th (1899–1901)	5
Populists	57th (1901–03)	5
Progressive Party (Roosevelt)	63rd (1913–15)	9
Progressive Party (Roosevelt)	64th (1915–17)	6
Progressive Party (Roosevelt)	65th (1917–19)	3
Progressive Party (La Follette)	74th (1935–36)	7
Progressive Party (La Follette)	75th (1937–38)	8
Progressive Party (La Follette)	76th (1939–40)	3

Senate

Third Party	Congress (Years)	# of Members
Liberal Republicans	43rd (1873–75)	7
Re-Adjusters	48th (1883–85)	2
Populists	52nd (1891–93)	2
Populists	53rd (1893–95)	3
Populists	54th (1895–97)	4
Silver Party	54th (1895–97)	2
Populists	55th (1897–99)	5
Silver Party	55th (1897–99)	2
Silver Republicans	55th (1897–99)	5
Populists	56th (1899–1901)	5
Silver Party	56th (1899–1901)	2
Silver Republicans	56th (1899–1901)	3
Populists	57th (1901–03)	2

the Senate, it nonetheless was active in running Senate candidates, and, Theodore Roosevelt the Party's candidate for president in 1912, was the last third party candidate to out poll a major party candidate, finishing second to Democrat Woodrow Wilson that year. This level of success in presidential politics and the extended time period in which the Roosevelt Progressives were represented in the House, leads one to believe that the Progressives might have been more successful in helping to secure landmark legislative achievement than third parties with lesser electoral accomplishment.[18]

Measuring Landmark Productivity

Having identified the instances of third party involvement in Congress, it is now necessary to determine what ought to be considered "landmark" laws. A database was constructed which draws on seven histories of Congress, the presidents, or the United States, and six encyclopedias on the same topics, and then adds two encyclopedias on American public policy. In all, 15 varied sources were consulted—a list of the sources consulted is provided as an Appendix to this chapter. Each of the 15 sources is readily available in most university libraries which can aid replication of this measurement strategy.[19]

Multiple and wide-ranging sources were used to provide a robust check on the importance of each law. The seven histories are read page-by-page and all new laws mentioned in the text of the histories are noted. With the encyclopedias, only the indexes are consulted, and again, each law mentioned is entered into the database. All entries were independently confirmed via multiple listings in the varied sources or by searching *Statues at Large* to ensure that the entry represented an enacted law. There are no treaties or independent executive branch actions included in the database.[20] The analysis reaches back to the 1st Congress (1789–91) and forward to the 103rd Congress (1993–94). In all, there are 1649 public laws or joint resolutions mentioned in the 15 sources, with 940 of the laws mentioned in more than one source. Only the Civil Rights Act of 1964 is mentioned in all 15 sources.[21]

During the time period covered by this research, the 43rd to the 76th Congresses, there are 480 laws to consider or laws that were mentioned in at least one of the sources. Being mentioned in only one source though is unlikely to be sufficient to be considered a landmark law. Hence, the research makes a qualitative judgment about the number of mentions necessary to judge a particular enactment as either notable or landmark. Specifically, if a law is mentioned three or more times these measures are referred to as *Notable Laws*. If the law is mentioned in five or more sources, at least one of which was in a Congress-specific publication, these are referred to as *Landmark Laws*. As noted, the sources consulted are varied and the requirement that one of the Congress-specific sources mentions the law is done to ensure that it has support from scholars of that branch of government. Five total sources are required to ensure that a law has broad visibility as a significant enactment.

Figure 4.2 exhibits the movement in legislative productivity from the 43 (1873–75) to the 76th (1939–40) Congresses. The dashed line represents the number of new notable laws passed in each Congress. There are 285 such enactments in the time period examined. The solid line represents

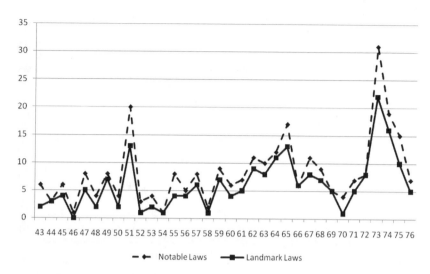

Figure 4.2 Notable and landmark legislative productivity by Congress: 43rd Congress (1873–75) to the 76th Congress (1939–40).

the number of new landmark laws by Congress and there are 207 of them during the relevant time period. Looking at Landmark Laws, in Figure 4.2, the four most productive Congresses are the 51st (1889–91), the 65th (1917–19), the 73rd (1933–35), and the 74th (1935–36). The latter two are President Franklin Roosevelt's first two New Deal Congresses. The 51st and 65th Congresses each produced 13 landmark acts and the two Roosevelt Congresses 22 and 16 landmark laws, respectively. Notably, the achievements of the 51st Congress, which included the Sherman Anti-Trust Act of 1890 and the McKinley Tariff Act of 1890, were not sustained and the 52nd Congress saw the enactment of only one additional landmark law. The 65th Congress, on the other hand, was part of an eight-year period covering four Congresses that each produced at least eight landmark pieces of legislation (the 62nd through the 65th Congresses).

Considering other productive Congresses, it should be noted that Roosevelt's success in the 73rd and 74th Congresses was preceded by a fruitful 72nd Congress, which had a Republican President (Herbert Hoover) and the Democratic Party controlled Congress. The 72nd Congress successfully proposed both the 20th and 21st Amendments to the United States Constitution, in addition to six other enactments that this research is considering landmark. The 75th Congress, Roosevelt's third, also witnessed considerable success, producing ten landmark acts. Hence, the period from 1931 to 1938, representing the last Hoover Congress and the first three Franklin Roosevelt Congresses, is also remarkable for sustained landmark productivity.

Table 4.2 Correlations between "Notable" and "Landmark" Legislative Production and an Existing Measure of Productivity by Congress

MEASURE	Notable	Landmark	Heitshusen/Young (43rd–76th)
Notable Laws	I	.97*** n = 34	.67** n = 34
Landmark Laws		I	.71** n = 34
Heitshusen/Young			I

*** p <.001; ** p <.01 (two-tailed test).

In order to get a handle on the validity of the measure of landmark productivity assembled for this research, values were compared to some existing measures that also count landmark legislative enactments. Table 4.2 presents a bivariate correlation between this measure of landmark laws and an existing measure assembled by Valerie Heitshusen and Garry Young,[22] as well as the correlation between what this research has labeled "Landmark Laws" and "Notable Laws." The intention is to provide some indication of the quality of the measure to be used in the analysis that follows. First, it can be noted in Table 4.2 that landmark laws and notable laws are very highly correlated, suggesting the two new measures are mutually confirming. Second, both indicators correlate reasonably well with the Heitshusen and Young measure during the relevant time period. Third, but not reported in the table because the relevant time period does not overlap, the measure of landmark laws developed for this work correlates even better with measures that have been created by Sarah Binder and David Mayhew that cover the post-World War II era.[23] The list of over 200 landmark laws from the time period covered by this research is available from the author.

In the case studies that follow, primary and secondary sources are consulted to learn the relevant legislative agenda of the eight third parties. Two of the eight parties identified—the Silver Party and the Silver Republican Party— had such a similar and limited legislative agenda that they are treated as one case in the investigation that follows. In the tables that conclude each case study, the legislative agenda of each third party is noted and whether there was action on the agenda item during the Congresses when the third party was actually present, but also whether there was legislative action in subsequent Congresses. The latter points to the possibility that third parties play an agenda setting role, but are not causal agents producing landmark laws in the manner prescribed in the introduction to this chapter. This would particularly be the case if the landmark achievement occurs in the distant future and not in a Congress that immediately follows the departure of the third party.

The Case Studies

To determine whether or not there is a correlation between the presence of third parties in Congress and landmark legislative productivity it is necessary to study the party platforms of the third parties. This correlation analysis, of course, is far from foolproof. It is very difficult to determine with certainty whether a third party had a causal influence on the passage of the landmark legislation. A correlation between the issues supported by third parties, and their members of Congress, and landmark pieces of legislation does not necessarily mean the third party played a significant role in the passage of the particular piece of legislation. However, in some instances, the research is able to advance causal claims based on articles from the *New York Times*, which suggest a direct role played by third parties or their members.[24] Moreover, in the discussion at the end of the case studies it will be shown that a reasonable interpretation of historical events suggests that the Populist Party may have moderated two-party legislative conflict when it was at extremely high levels, while the Progressive Party in the Woodrow Wilson Administration increased issue salience and effectively worked to help define a legislative agenda when two-party struggle had been waning.

Liberal Republican Party

The Liberal Republican Party managed to hold four seats in the House of Representatives and seven Senate seats in the 43rd Congress (1873–75). The party was formally organized in 1872 in Cincinnati, Ohio, although there were some activities by those who formally initiated the party dating back to 1870, in Missouri. The Liberal Republican Party's initial objective was the defeat of Ulysses S. Grant as president of the United States in the 1872 presidential election. Members of the party felt that Grant and the Republican Party's platform, which included measures arguably intended to punish Southern states, were too radical.[25]

Among the early supporters of the Liberal Republican Party were newspaper editors, several with significant influence—including Horace White from the *Chicago Tribune*, Murat Halstead from the *Cincinnati Commercial*, Horace Greeley from the *New York Times*, and former Senator and Secretary of the Interior Carl Schurz from the *Detroit Post*. Each felt that the goals of Reconstruction had been achieved and therefore national government troops should be withdrawn from the South.[26]

At the party's first convention in Cincinnati in 1872, a platform was approved which called for civil service reform to curtail Grant's authority over executive branch officers, restoration of voting and office-holding rights for former citizens of the Confederacy, and removal of national government troops from the South. At the Convention, the party nominated Horace Greeley as its presidential candidate and chose other members to run for seats in Congress.[27]

Table 4.3 Liberal Republican Party and Landmark Legislation, 1873–1875

Platform Items	Landmark Law Passed in Current Congress	Landmark Law Passed by Subsequent Congress
Civil Service Reform	No	Civil Service Act of 1883 (ch. 27, Stat. 403)
Troop Withdrawal from the South	No	^
Restoration of Ex-Confederate Office-Holding Rights	No	^

Notes

^ These actions were taken but are not considered a landmark legislative accomplishment, as defined by this research.

Many of those nominated to run for House and Senate seats ran as fusion candidates with the Democratic Party. In many instances, the two parties cooperated in a significant manner with each nominating half of the slate of candidates for a given state.[28] Despite this, the Liberal Republican's success in elections that year was marginal. Greeley won only a handful of states in the presidential election and following his death late in November of 1872, the party fell apart and saw no success in subsequent national elections.[29]

As has often been the case with short-lived third parties, the platform of the Liberal Republican Party was quite limited. There are really only three issues that were raised at the Party's first and only national convention. Table 4.3 lists the issues or policy positions of the Liberal Republican Party and subsequent legislative action on these matters. Notably, there was no movement on any of the three issues in the Congress when the Liberal Republicans actually held seats. Though, within a period of ten years, one of the three issues was addressed by a landmark law.[30] Specifically, the civil service reform advocated by the Liberal Republican Party was realized in 1883.

Nationals (Greenback Party)

The Nationals, also known as the Greenback Party, rose to prominence in American politics in the decade that spanned the mid-1870s to the mid-1880s. The party won 13 seats in the House of Representatives in the 1878 elections and followed this up with ten victories in the 1880 elections. The party also controlled local governments in the state of Ohio; however, it never gained representation in the United States Senate. The National's initial platform was focused on issues regarding monetary policies and national currency. The term "Greenbacks" is a reference to paper notes used during and after the Civil War that were legal tender but were not backed by any specie such as gold or silver. Following the depression of 1873, known as the Panic of 1873, which hurt farming interests in particular, there was significant debate regarding the future of the paper notes or "greenbacks." The Nationals wanted to put more greenbacks into circulation to take financial pressure off farmers and others in economic peril.[31]

The party held six national nominating conventions between 1874 and 1888; their last convention in 1888, however, was attended by only eight delegates and no candidates were nominated. At the 1878 Convention, the party developed a platform that included the monetization of silver, a repeal of the National Banking Act of 1863, and repeal of the Species Resumption Act of 1875, which was intended to reinstate or "resume" the gold standard and take greenbacks out of circulation.[32] For the 1880 elections, the party expanded its platform to focus attention on social and labor issues. For instance, the Nationals came out in support of a national income tax, an eight-hour work day, and women's suffrage. This move was an attempt to broaden support for the party and especially for their 1880 presidential candidate, James Weaver from Iowa. In the 1880 presidential contest, Weaver gained just over 305,000 votes, representing 3.3 percent of votes cast.[33]

Following the 1880 elections, the Nationals began to lose significant support, especially to the Democratic Party. Yet many of the Nationals would later participate in other third parties, most notably the Populist Party.[34] From Table 4.4 one can see that the Nationals did not achieve much contemporaneous legislative success. The repeal of the Species Resumption Act of 1875 never occurred. Nonetheless, the Bland Allison Act of 1878 did provide for the coinage of some additional silver dollars, which was helpful to farmers backing the Nationals because it increased the overall money supply making it easier for them to meet their debt obligations. Importantly, this landmark act was passed after the Nationals had formed as a third party but before they actually gained representation in Congress. Hence, it is not counted as a third

Table 4.4 Greenback Party (Nationals) and Landmark Legislation, 1879–1883

Platform Items	Landmark Law Passed in Current Congress	Landmark Law Passed by Subsequent Congress
Free Coinage of Silver	No	No
Repeal of the National Bank Act	No	No
Repeal of The Species Resumption Act of 1875	No	No
National Income Tax	No	Wilson-Gorman Tariff Act (ch. 349, Stat. 570); Sixteenth Amendment to the U.S. Constitution
Eight-Hour Work Day	No	Fair Labor Standards Act of 1938 (P.L. 75–718)
Women's Suffrage	No	Nineteenth Amendment to the U.S. Constitution

party legislative success by this research. Several of the party's broader issue concerns, including support for an income tax, eight-hour work days, and women's suffrage, were eventually addressed by landmark laws during the first decades of the twentieth century.

Readjuster Party

The Readjuster Party was founded in Virginia following the Civil War and placed four members in the House of Representatives and two members in the Senate, all from Virginia, in the 48th Congress (1883–85). During the post-Civil War era, Virginia politicians were caught in a heated debate regarding the state's responsibility for debt incurred during the war. The Readjuster faction was strongly in favor of a reduction in the amount of debt that Virginia would be responsible for, specifically the portion of the debt that was incurred reconstructing the infrastructure destroyed during the war.[35] In addition, it can be noted that the Readjusters were a biracial political party and supported efforts to promote and preserve the political rights of former slaves. The party successfully elected two former slaves to the Richmond, Virginia school board in the 1880s.[36]

From Table 4.5 one can note that in addition to supporting the readjustment of Virginia's war debt, the Readjuster Party supported national government funding for public education and the repeal of the poll tax.[37] Like other local and short-lived third parties, the Readjusters did not enjoy any contemporaneous landmark legislative success. Even so, two of the three issues that it championed were eventually addressed by Congress and became landmark enactments. Within ten years of the Readjuster Party's call for national government funding for public education, Congress made a foray into national government support for public education with the Morrill Land Grant College Act of 1890. The Act provided national government land for state colleges focused on agriculture and mechanical arts education. A second Morrill Act in 1890 required each state to show that race was not an admissions criterion or

Table 4.5 Readjuster Party and Landmark Legislation, 1883–1885

Platform Items	Landmark Law Passed in Current Congress	Landmark Law Passed by Subsequent Congress
Readjustment of Virginia's War Debt	No	No
Support for Public Education	No	Morrill Land-Grant College Act (P.L. 51–249)
Repeal of the Poll Tax	No	Twenty-fourth Amendment to the U.S. Constitution

else to designate a separate land-grant institution for persons of color. It is not difficult to imagine that the Readjuster Party's position on race was part of the momentum that contributed to the passage of landmark legislation on public education for all. The poll tax was not repealed until 1964, so it is quite clear that the Readjuster Party did not have direct causal involvement. But it does support the notion of third parties bringing issues to the country's attention that are ultimately addressed by Congress.

Populist Party

For a 12-year period spanning 1891 to 1903 the Populist Party was able to seat members in both chambers of the United States Congress. In the 55th Congress (1897–99) there were 22 Populist Party members in the House of Representatives representing a little over 6 percent of total membership. In both the 55th and 56th Congress (1897–1901) there were five Populist Party members in the Senate, representing 5.6 percent of that chamber. One might imagine that these elevated levels of third party representation might be more meaningfully associated with landmark legislative productivity.

The Populist Party originated in the mid- to late 1870s, representing farming interests in Western states. A primary policy concern was falling prices on agricultural commodities.[38] The party was first called the Farmer's Alliance, and effective leadership caused the group to expand in influence. Ultimately, the group merged with the National Agricultural Wheel and expanded its geographic coverage and influence to Southern and Midwestern states.[39] The group first elected members to Congress in the 1890 midterm elections, although it was not yet known as the Populist Party. The Alliance held a series of national conferences in 1892, which resulted in the formation of the Populist Party, also known as the People's National Party.[40] At the party's first national convention, held that same year, party leaders adopted what today is known as the Omaha Platform. The major planks in the platform were a call for a graduated national income tax, the unlimited coinage of silver in opposition to a gold standard, direct election of United States senators, adoption of the Australian ballot, a term limit for the United States president, an eight-hour work day for government employees, opposition to the national bank, civil service reform, limits on immigration, and passage of a system to allow for direct democracy in the form of referenda and ballot initiatives.[41]

The party was able to maintain membership in six consecutive Congresses and many Populist Party candidates were aided by fusion practices, which allowed members to run both as a Populist and as either a Democrat or a Republican Party candidate.[42] In the South, Populists fused with the Republican Party and in other regions with the Democratic Party. There were also marginally successful Populist Party presidential candidates during this time period. James B. Weaver, who previously ran for president as a member of the Greenback Party, was nominated as the Populist Party's candidate for president 1892. Weaver was able to win Electoral College votes from four states and slightly over one million popular votes. William Jennings Bryan, the Democratic nominee for president in 1896, was also nominated by the Populist Party. Despite this fusion presidential ticket, the Republican Party nominee William McKinley won the election. In spite of this, the Populist Party was able to seat 22 members in the House of Representatives as a result of the 1896 election.

It had been speculated that this higher level of third party exposure to national politics and the legislative process ought to associate with more landmark legislative achievement. Indeed, this is the case. Table 4.6 spells out the ten issues that made up the Omaha Platform. Of these, two of them were addressed by landmark laws while the Populists were in Congress. A third and fourth issue, the eight-hour work day for government employees and civil service reform, were addressed by new laws but these enactments do not reach landmark status as defined by this research. Two additional legislative matters, the adoption of the Australian ballot and the adoption of direct democracy procedures, also occurred during the period that the Populist Party was prominent in American politics. However, both of these issues dealt with matters

Table 4.6 Populist Party and Landmark Legislation, 1891–1903

Platform Items	Landmark Law Passed in Current Congress	Landmark Law Passed by Subsequent Congress
Income Tax Reform	Wilson-Gorman Tariff Act (ch. 349, Stat. 570)	Sixteenth Amendment to the U.S. Constitution
Free Coinage of Silver	No	No
Direct Election of Senators	No	Seventeenth Amendment to the U.S. Constitution
Adoption of Australian Ballot	*	*
Term Limit for the President	No	Twenty-second Amendment to the U.S. Constitution
Eight-Hour Work Day for Gov. Employees	No	Fair Labor Standards Act (PL 75–718)
No National Bank	No	No
Civil Service Reform	No	Many alterations in subsequent years
Limits on Immigration	Geary Chinese Exclusion Act (P.L. 47–71, ch. 126); Immigration Act of 1903 (ch. 32, Stat. 1213)	Creation of the Bureau of Immigration and Naturalization in 1906 (P.L. 59–338)
Direct Democracy Initiatives	*	*

* Passed by many state legislatures.

relating to state law and consequently were not addressed by the United States Congress. In all, six of the ten Omaha Platform policy issues saw legislative action during the 12-year period that the Populist Party was most important. Two additional policies, the direct election of senators and a term limit for the United States president, were addressed by constitutional amendments in subsequent years.

Of the ten Populist platform items only the free coinage of silver and the elimination of the national bank have never seen any legislative action. Moreover, it is quite common for American history books to point out the relationship between the Populist Party and the passage of the Wilson–Gorman Tariff of 1894, suggesting a causal relationship between the party's platform issue and the passage of the first peacetime income tax.[43] This particular legislation was overturned on the Supreme Court as unconstitutional, but less than ten years after the Populist had left Congress, the national government income tax was supported by the passage of the Sixteenth Amendment to the Constitution.

Silver Party and Silver Republican Party

Although the origins of the Silver Party and the Silver Republican Party are somewhat distinct, each existed in roughly the same time period and had the same core policy concern. Specifically the Silver Party's origins can be traced to the state of Nevada during the 1890s. In the years following the Civil War, Nevada, along with other Western states and territories, were the center of silver mining in the United States. This was of particular importance as silver was used in currency. But, due to the influx of silver into the market and the fear of a decrease in market prices, silver was demonetized in 1873, which resulted in a significant outcry by Silver Barons and the public in these Western areas.[44]

As a result, people in Nevada began organizing a Silver Party, which had considerable success in local government beginning in 1892. The only congressional representation obtained by the Silver Party, however, was two United States Senate seats from Nevada following the 1894 midterm election. These two members completed their six-year terms giving the Silver Party representation in three Congresses (54th–56th). Following the completion of these Senate terms, the Silver Party saw its success dwindle, with little nationwide or even statewide accomplishments after 1902.[45]

At the same time, the Silver Republican Party arose from a philosophical split within the Republican Party over the gold standard. Like the Silver Party, the Silver Republican Party's influence was centered primarily in Western mining states where silver mining was of particular economic importance. The party elected three members to the House of the Representatives and five members to the Senate in the 1896 elections. All five senators, however,

Table 4.7 Silver Party/Silver Republican Party and Landmark Legislation, 1895–1901

Platform Items	Landmark Law Passed in Current Congress	Landmark Law Passed by Subsequent Congress
Free Coinage of Silver	No	No

returned their allegiance to the Republican Party before the end of their six-year terms.

The Silver Party held a national nominating convention in 1896 and wrote a party platform. The document is not particularly lengthy, but does indicate their intention to spell out the party's issue positions in detail.[46] Yet, all discussion in the platform document is centered on the issue of monetary policy and, specifically, the establishment of a bimetallic standard, whereby silver and gold would both be used to back currency. Secondary sources suggest the Silver Republican Party was also focused on only one issue, the free coinage of silver.[47] Table 4.7 shows that there was no significant movement on the bimetallic or silver issue during the time period that the two third parties saw representation in Congress, nor in subsequent Congresses.

The Silver Purchase Act of 1890, which is considered a landmark law by this research, passed before the silver parties gained representation in the United States Congress. An amendment to the Gold Standard Act of 1900, another piece of legislation that this research has labeled landmark, sponsored by Henry Moore Teller (Silver-Republican-CO) calling for an international bimetallic standard was rejected by a wide margin in the Senate.[48] In December 1899, Congress passed another Silver Purchase Act, but this legislation, which did receive the support of members of both silver parties, was only mentioned in one of the 15 sources consulted by this research and is not deemed even a "notable" legislative achievement.

Progressive Party (Roosevelt)

A split in the Republican Party between President William Howard Taft and former President Theodore Roosevelt led to the creation of the Progressive Party of 1912, also known as the Bull Moose Party. Roosevelt had broken with Taft around 1911 and sought the Republican nomination for president in 1912. Following Taft's success at the Republican National Convention, Roosevelt left the party and created the Progressive Party to run candidates at both the state and national level.[49] Table 4.8 outlines the platform adopted at the party's first national convention in August 1912. The foundation of the document was centered on a philosophy known as New Nationalism, which emphasized that a strong national government was necessary to protect individual rights and to ensure proper regulation of the economy.[50]

Table 4.8 Progressive Party (Roosevelt) and Landmark Legislation, 1913–1919

Platform Items	Landmark Law Passed in Current Congress	Landmark Law Passed by Subsequent Congress
Women's Suffrage	No	Nineteenth Amendment to the U.S. Constitution
Mandatory Health Insurance	No	Patient Protection and Affordable Care Act (P.L. 111–148)
Income Tax Reform (post-16th Amendment)	Revenue Act of 1913 (P.L. 63–16); Revenue Act of 1916 (P.L. 64–271); Excess Profits Tax of 1917 (P.L. 65–63) Revenue Act of 1918 (P.L. 65–254);	n/a
Labor Union Rights	Clayton Anti-Trust Act (P.L. 63–212)	n/a
Child Labor Laws	Keating–Owen Child Labor Act (P.L. 64–249)	n/a
Farm Relief	Smith–Lever Act (ch. 79, Stat. 372); Federal Farm Loan Bank Act (ch. 245, Stat. 382)	n/a
Inheritance Taxes	∧	Many alterations in subsequent years
Direct Election of Senators	Seventeenth Amendment to the U.S. Constitution	n/a
Primary Elections	*	*
Recall Judicial Decisions	No	No
Direct Democracy Provisions	*	*
Public Control of Utilities	*	Public Utility Holding Company Act of 1935 (P.L. 74–333)
Worker's Compensation Insurance	*	*
Financial Regulation	Federal Reserve Bank Act (P.L. 63–43); Federal Trade Commission Act (P.L. 63–203)	n/a
Campaign Finance Reform	No	Federal Elections Campaign Act (P.L. 92–225)
Registration of Lobbyists	No	Federal Regulation of Lobbying Act (P.L. 79–601)
Making Congressional Committee Hearings Public	No	#

Notes

∧ Estate Tax of 1916 passes in the 64th Congress, but is not considered a landmark legislative accomplishment, as defined by this research.

* Passed by many state legislatures.

Beginning in 1979 the House of Representatives began televising committee hearings.

Roosevelt was able to garner 27 percent of the popular vote in the 1912 presidential election compared to only 23 percent for the incumbent President Taft. This is the only instance since the Civil War of a third party presidential candidate receiving more votes than a major party candidate.[51] Some argue that the defeat of Roosevelt and other Progressives was attributable to both the unity of the Democratic Party and the progressive nature of Wilson's platform.[52] Furthermore, the Bull Moose Party had significant funding issues complicated by the party's effort to elect candidates at both state and national levels.[53] Even with these hurdles, the Roosevelt Progressive Party manages to swear in nine members of the House of Representatives in 1913.[54]

Roosevelt lost the election of 1912, but the same cannot be said for many of the ideas and issue positions supported by the Progressive Party of 1912. The issues enumerated in Table 4.8 are likely familiar to all readers, many of the same topics are debated in Congress today, suggesting that the party was truly "progressive" in its policy positions. In all, the Progressive Party platform in 1912 outlined 17 different issue positions. Of these, six saw legislative action while the Progressive Party members were seated in the House of Representatives. One of the issues, income tax reform, witnessed four new landmark laws during the three Congresses in which the party held seats. In addition, there were two new landmark laws that addressed farm relief and financial regulation—other Progressive Party planks. In all, 11 new landmark laws addressing six Progressive Party topics passed during the brief stint the party was in Congress.

Many other Roosevelt Progressive Party issues were addressed by state legislation and laws that this research does not consider landmark. Indeed, only one of the 17 different issues on the 1912 Progressive Party platform has never received any legislative attention either by the national legislature or by state governments. That issue is the recall of judicial decisions, which would have allowed the people to vote to repeal the decisions made by judges.

In the 63rd and 64th Congresses, nearly one-third of all landmark laws passed are correlated with the Progressive Party's 1912 platform, including implementation of income taxes, early efforts to regulate child labor, rights for labor unions, and significant financial regulatory reforms that led to the creation of the Federal Reserve System and the Federal Trade Commission. Moreover, members of the Progressive Party played a role in writing some of this legislation, and the Federal Trade Commission Act was sponsored by Progressive Party Representative Victor Murdock of Kansas.

President Woodrow Wilson acknowledged the significance of the Progressive Party in landmark legislative achievements. Wilson noted that in the 1912 elections the Democratic Party platform did not actively advocate for child labor restrictions or a Federal Reserve; however, after the Progressive Party "sharply call[ed] the attention of the people to these needed measures," the issues were ultimately taken up by the Democratic Party and passed.[55] This direct acknowledgment by the president of third party influence on the passage of landmark acts cannot be ignored, nor should it be. The Progressive Party of 1912 had very minimal representation in Congress, but it occurred at a time when the two major parties were not distinguishing themselves in a major way,[56] an environment where one might expect a third party to be able to assist the structuring of conflict and policy options.

Progressive Party (La Follette)

The efforts of the two sons of former Wisconsin Senator and presidential candidate Robert La Follette, Sr. led to the creation of the La Follette Progressive Party in the midst of the Great Depression. Philip La Follette and Robert La Follette, Jr. created the party in 1934 in an attempt to seek both statewide and national offices; however, the party was initially focused on Wisconsin state politics. The new Progressive Party's main supporters consisted of progressive-minded members of Wisconsin's Republican Party, members of organized labor throughout the Midwest, and major farm organizations across the state of Wisconsin.[57] The party did not gain representation in the United States Senate, but did seat a minimum of three members in the House of Representatives for three consecutive Congresses: the 74th through the 76th. The highest representation total was eight members of the House in the 75th Congress.

At the party's first convention in May 1934 the platform written included many Roosevelt Progressive Party issues such as income tax reform, the right of labor unions to organize, and public ownership of utilities. The new Progressive Party also called for a program of unemployment insurance, financial aid to homeowners, old-age pensions, and public approval of war via referendum. At the heart of the La Follette Progressive Party agenda though was a focus on agricultural issues, specifically ensuring that farmers were guaranteed a profit on their investments.[58]

One can see from Table 4.9, like the first Progressive Party, there is a strong correlation between the La Follette Progressive Party's stated platform issues and landmark legislative achievement. Moreover, much of the achievement is contemporaneous or takes place while the party members are seated in Congress. Of the eight issues associated with the new Progressive Party, only "approval of war via referendum" has never received any legislative attention. Three of the eight issues, including the rights of labor unions, public ownership of utilities, and farm assistance each are addressed by multiple landmark acts while the party is in Congress. Because many of these issues were supported by Democrats and Republicans as well as the Progressives, it is difficult to make a direct causal link to the third party. However, the theory elaborated at the beginning of the chapter was not about actual sponsorship of legislation but instead about the possibility that the mere presence of third parties might moderate conflict, lowering it when party polarization is high and raising it

Table 4.9 Progressive Party (La Follette) and Landmark Legislation, 1935–1941

Platform Items	Landmark Law Passed in Current Congress	Landmark Law Passed by Subsequent Congress
Income Tax Reform	No	Many alterations in subsequent years
Labor Union Rights	National Labor Relations Act (P.L. 74–198); Fair Labor Standards Act (P.L. 75–718)	n/a
Public Ownership of Utilities	Public Utility Holding Company Act of 1935 (P.L. 74–333)	n/a
Unemployment Insurance	Social Security Act of 1935 (P.L. 74–271)	n/a
Homeowner Financial Aid	Wagner–Steagall Housing Act (P.L. 75–412)	n/a
Old-Age Pensions	Social Security Act of 1935 (P.L. 74–271)	n/a
Approval of War via Referendum	No	No
Farming Assistance	Frazier–Lemke Farm Mortgage Moratorium Act (P.L. 73–486); Soil Conservation and Domestic Allotment Act (P.L. 74–46); Agricultural Adjustment Act (P.L. 75–430)	n/a

when polarization dips. This issue will now be investigated more completely in the discussion that follows.

Discussion

It is likely the case that three House members or two members of the Senate is too low a threshold for meaningful third party involvement in the legislative process. Moreover, it would now seem after studying the Liberal Republican and Readjuster Parties that third party representation in a single Congress is not sufficient to influence the contemporaneous legislative process in a significant manner. However, it may be the case that this kind of minimal third party representation can help establish forthcoming legislative agendas in a meaningful way. Both third parties, present in only a single Congress, advocated for changes that were not ignored by future Congresses. Focusing on a single issue, as was the case with the Silver Party and the Silver Republican Party, also does not foretell meaningful legislative involvement for third parties.

What is now clear is that when third parties have more than a couple of members in Congress who retain seats for longer than two years and advocate a more complete legislative agenda, they are associated with landmark legislative accomplishment. When third parties such as the Populists and Progressives have managed to hold seats for more than two consecutive Congresses, their platform positions have been enacted both in contemporaneous Congresses and in succeeding Congresses. Moreover, the new laws associated with these third parties represent more than incremental change. The policy changes associated with these third parties have found their way into general history books and encyclopedias.

The minimal level of third party representation and the duration of third party representation in Congress necessary to produce legislative achievement is a question that this research will not be able to answer. Yet, the hope was to go further than to simply identify association between third party representation in Congress and landmark laws. The hope was that one might be able to extract some basis for making a causal claim regarding the presence of third parties in Congress and productivity. In order to do this it is necessary to return again to the issue of major party polarization.

Existing research has made the case and provided empirical evidence to support the notion that moderate levels of major party polarization are most productive.[59] Now it becomes necessary to determine whether third parties can help moderate conflict—reducing tensions when major party conflict is too high and raising the level of conflict when the two parties are failing to distinguish themselves or provide a meaningful policy agenda. Figure 4.3 plots the level of major party polarization in the time period studied in this chapter.

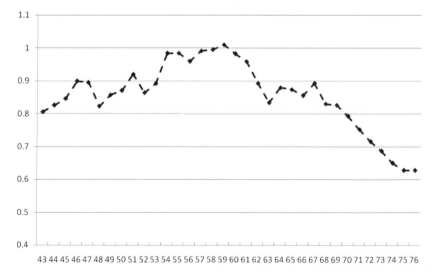

Figure 4.3 Two-chamber average level of major party polarization, by Congress.

The chart uses data supplied by Keith Poole, who uses a form of factor analysis to derive an indicator of the distinctiveness of the voting behavior of each individual member of Congress.[60] This research averages the individual values to create political party specific scores and then calculates the absolute value of the difference of the two major parties' values. This is done separately for each chamber of Congress; however, because the two chamber averages are so highly correlated during the time period of the study ($r = .97$), the chamber values are simply averaged.

Going forward it makes most sense to focus on the Populist Party and the Roosevelt Progressive Party when attempting to determine whether third parties were able to moderate conflict. The first had representation in six consecutive Congresses and in both chambers of the legislature. The second saw representation in three consecutive Congresses and was lead by a former president who polled very well in the 1912 presidential election as a third party candidate. These are the two parties in this analysis that obtained a reasonable level of sustained and salient electoral success.

Examining Figure 4.3 one can notice that polarization, or major party voting distinctiveness, was at a very high level when the Populist Party had members in the nation's legislature: the 52nd through 57th Congresses. The 1890s and the turn into the 20th century are known to have experienced some of the most disciplined major political parties in the country's history, and the time period is defined by extraordinary powerful leaders in both major political parties.[61] James Sundquist notes the time period reached a "historic high point in the degree of internal [party] discipline, [which] it achieved behind strong leaders."[62] If the Populist Party members were going to be causal agents producing landmark laws in this political environment, they would have to reduce major party tension.

Most notably, this time period is characterized by disappearing quorums and other tactics used by the minority party to stymie majority party accomplishment. Some of the strongest party leaders the House of Representatives has likely ever known, men such as Thomas B. Reed (R-ME), Charles Crisp (D-GA), and Joseph G. Cannon (R-IL), served alongside the Populist Party members in the Lower Chamber. These were major party leaders that knew the ins and outs of obstructionism.

It has been noted that the Populist Party had 22 members in the House of Representatives in the 55th Congress (1897–99). Most of these Populist Party members ran under fusion practices that allowed them to run as both a member of the Populist Party and as either a Democrat or a Republican. Outside of the South, Populist candidates represented the Democratic Party in opposition to a Republican Party candidate. In Southern states such as Alabama, North Carolina, Tennessee, and Texas the Populist Party candidates were successful in representing both their party and the Republican Party against Democrats. In all, the Populist Party legislators serving in the late 1890s had considerable cross-major party allegiances. Given this, it is not too difficult to imagine that their presence and voices during legislative debate would serve a moderating influence.

The extent of the Populist Party cross-major party loyalty was not limited to electoral campaigns. The party had considerable cross-regional adherents as well, representing states in the South, Midwest, and West. The South was considered a Democratic Party stronghold and the West and Midwest were Republican regions. This geographic coverage by the Populists in Congress had to serve to check sectionalism, to some degree, a phenomenon that has been related to major party conflict.

The Party's members also sided with different major political parties on policy, depending on the issue being considered. On monetary policy the Democrats became willing to side with the Populist call for free coinage of silver in the 1896 presidential campaign. Populist Party calls for a secret ballot and direct democracy initiatives resonated more strongly with Republican Party leaders. The Populist Party's stand on income tax reform had supporters and detractors in both major political parties and the same can be said for limits on immigration. In all, the party could hardly fuel major party conflict when its stand on the issues crossed party lines so readily.

The Populist served during a time period when Congress, and the country, was going to witness a major realignment of the major parties so there was plenty of instances when individual members of the major parties agreed with one another, but in the aggregate, the parties were disciplined and antagonistic. The presence of Populists who shared their views, representing regions of the country that were considered their stronghold, and running for office as fusion candidates under their party label could not cause more tension or major party conflict. Moreover, the simple fact that Populist Party members were not consistently siding with either major party had to cause major party leaders and followers to moderate. In a period of intense major party discipline, and rivalry, the Populist Party's presence in Congress cooled partisan rhetoric and prompted compromising sentiments. It is this moderation of legislative conflict this research suggests that led the Populist Party to be associated with both contemporaneous and ensuing landmark legislative accomplishment.

Turning to the Roosevelt Progressive Party, although it never achieved representation in the Senate, it did experience relative success in electing members to the House of Representatives and provided a viable option in the presidential elections of both 1912 and 1916. Importantly, the Progressives were able to maintain minimum representation in the House of Representatives for three successive Congresses. Specifically, the Roosevelt Progressives were represented in the 63rd–65th Congresses. An examination of Figure 4.3 shows the time period is characterized by falling levels of major party polarization. The 63rd Congress (1913–15), the Progressives first in the House, witnessed the lowest level of polarization in a 28-year span dating back to the 48th Congress (1883–85).

Unlike the Populist Party, the Roosevelt Progressive Party was clearly more aligned with one of the major parties. The Party was an offshoot of the Republican Party and drew nearly all of its electoral support from former Republican Party members during its six-year run in Congress and national politics. It is important to recognize the single major party alliance experienced by the Progressive Party. If it is the case that the Populist Party's cross-party allegiances attenuated conflict when it was high, then it would make sense for the Progressive Party to be aligned with one if the intention is to argue that they are associated with increased conflict, sufficient to effectively define legislative policy strategies and policy options.

Moreover, if one wishes to suggest that Progressive Party presence in Congress had a causal relationship to landmark productivity during a period of relative low conflict, it will be important to show that the party was effective at agenda setting. Recall, from earlier in the chapter, the problem of low major party conflict is ineffective structuring of policy options and weak leaders. The third party in this scenario must be able to prompt immediate attention to problems that the major parties recognize, but have been unwilling to push, due in part to their own intra-party differences. Writing about the presidential platforms of the two major parties in 1912, E.E. Schattschneider notes their amazing level of congruence.[63] If the Roosevelt Progressives in the 1910s were going to cause landmark legislative innovation, they would have to help foster major party policy difference and policy structuring.

We have already seen that the Roosevelt Progressives did precisely this. *New York Times* articles from this period note President Wilson's acceptance that the Progressive Party deserved credit for calling the attention of the people to measures as diverse as child labor regulation and financial reform. The president's sentiments were echoed by Democratic National Committee Chairman Vance McCormick. The major party leader suggested legislative accomplishments such as additional income taxes, the Federal Reserve Act, Federal Trade Commission Act, the eight-hour work day, creation of a children's bureau, and additional anti-trust acts are all examples of the Democratic Party following the commitments of the Bull Moose Party platform of 1912.[64] It is clear that the Progressive Party played a major role in landmark legislative accomplishment during their brief time in Congress, primarily by establishing meaningful policy prescriptions for the two major parties to consider.

Interestingly, the Progressive Party success comes in Congresses when the major party they were most closely aligned with, electorally, is in the minority. It was President Wilson and the Democrats that took up Roosevelt's progressive agenda. The Roosevelt agenda stirred legislative malaise and increased issue salience and the majority was forced to react. Given declining major party distinctiveness in this time period, the majority party in Congress was willing to grab hold of third party ideas, establish a legislative agenda, and effect significant policy accomplishment.

Conclusion

Considering the history of eight third parties that obtained a minimal level of representation in Congress in the post-Civil War era it is possible to identify 37 wholly unique agenda items. Of these issue positions, 15 or over 40 percent were addressed by new landmark laws while the third party was seated in Congress. An additional ten issues were addressed by landmark laws in subsequent Congresses. No less than five constitutional amendments in the 20th century (the 16th, 17th, 19th, 22nd, and 24th) were passed after being advocated by a third party in the last decades of the 19th century. It is clearly the case that third party representation in Congress is neither a necessary nor a sufficient condition to produce major legislative change. However, it is also the case, when third party support for major change has occurred it does not hurt or prevent the adoption of landmark laws.

Assigning causality is forever a tricky matter. There is always the possibility that other considerations are intervening and corrupting the validity of a correlation analysis. The fact that third parties are neither a necessary nor a sufficient condition to produce landmark legislative achievement complicates matters. There are obviously a myriad of explanations for legislative accomplishment. In order to try to address this issue head on, this research champions a theory regarding the configuration of legislative conflict that would be most conducive to landmark productivity. Specifically, this research advocates the notion that moderate major party conflict will be most productive. Too little and you have the possibility of major party collusion to avoid pressing issues, too much and there is no room for major party compromise. Third parties, for their part, must moderate conflict to affect a causal claim.

There have been two third parties that have been significant electoral threats to the major parties in the post-Civil War United States: the Populist Party of the late 19th century and the Bull Moose Progressive Party in the second decade of the 20th century. In each instance the party platforms of these third parties can easily be correlated with landmark legislative enactments. Moving further to claim a causal relationship requires adherence to the notion espoused in this research about the role of moderate conflict. Observers of Congress will likely not quibble with the contention there was intense major party conflict when the Populists were in Congress. Likewise, observers will easily accept that high level of inter-party similarity, and consequently less inter-party conflict, existed when the Progressive Party seated nine members in the House of Representatives after the 1912 election. What is left is to decide whether the Populists might have moderated conflict and whether the Progressives might have awakened melancholy major parties, thus prompting significant legislative action. A review of the history of these two time periods suggests this is likely the case.

Appendix: Source Codebook—Landmark Legislation Project

Congressional Histories

Christianson, Stephen G. 1996. *Facts about the Congress.* New York: The H.W. Wilson Company.
Landsberg, Brian K., ed. 2004. "Timeline." in *Major Acts of Congress:* Gale Virtual Reference Library. 3 volumes. New York: Macmillan Reference USA.
Remini, Robert V. 2006. *The House: The History of the House of Representatives.* New York: Harper Collins Books.
Stathis, Stephen W. 2003. *Landmark Legislation, 1774–2002: Major U.S. Acts and Treaties.* Washington, DC: CQ Press.

Congressional Encyclopedias

Bacon, Donald C., Roger H. Davidson, and Morton Keller, eds. 1995. *The Encyclopedia of the United States Congress.* New York: Simon & Schuster.
DewHirst, Robert E. 2007. *Encyclopedia of the United States Congress.* New York: Facts on Files Inc.
Tarr, David R. and Ann O'Connor, eds. 1999. *Congress A-Z.* 3rd Ed. Washington, DC: CQ Press.

Presidential Histories

Jewell, Elizabeth. 2005. *U.S. Presidents Fact Book.* New York: Random House Reference.
Kane, Joseph Nathan. 1998. *Presidential Fact Book.* New York: Random House, Inc.

Presidential Encyclopedias

Levy, Leonard W., and Louis Fisher, eds. 1994. *Encyclopedia of the American Presidency.* New York: Simon & Shuster.
Nelson, Michael, ed. 1992. *CQ's Encyclopedia of American Government: The Presidency A to Z.* Washington, DC: Congressional Quarterly Inc.

American History

ABC-Clio. 2007. *America: History and Life.* http://www.abc-clio.com/products/serials_ahl.aspx (last accessed August 29, 2010).

American Encyclopedia

Finkleman, Paul, and Peter Wallenstein. 2001. *The Encyclopedia of American Political History.* Washington, DC: CQ Press.

Public Policy Encyclopedias

Jackson, Byron M. 1999. *Encyclopedia of American Public Policy.* Santa Barbara, CA: ABC-CLIO.

Rabin, Jack, ed. 2003. *Encyclopedia of Public Administration and Public Policy.* New York: Marcel Dekker, Inc.

Chapter 5

Third Parties and Civic Engagement

If liberty and equality, as is thought by some, are chiefly to be found in democracy, they will be best attained when all persons alike share in government to the utmost.

Aristotle

The objective of this chapter is to explore the consequences of two-party dominance as it relates to civic engagement and, more specifically, citizen political participation in the form of voting. Do viable third party candidates on the ballot link to higher voter turnout rates in the United States? Presumably, practicable third parties can energize the electoral environment and prompt higher levels of citizen participation. In addition to close scrutiny of the relationship between third parties and voter turnout, this chapter will provide the results of a test measuring the association between each American state's degree of third party voting and their level of citizen-interest group activity. The specific hypothesis is that the states most likely to support third party presidential candidates are more likely to have an engaged citizenry—defined as greater citizen-interest group density.

An obvious assumption being made is that greater citizen engagement is a good idea. Aristotle's line of reasoning notwithstanding, there has been academic debate over the virtues of expanding citizen participation. On the one hand, scholars doubt the practicality and prudence of increased citizen participation. They recognize the public is less than perfectly informed and that the public's political views are often unrestrained by ideology, carelessly constructed, and do not comport well with real world happenings.[1] Others suggest that voters and non-voters are not appreciably different and consequently non-participation has no detrimental effects.[2] Still more, there are candidates running for public office who hope their opponent's supporters do not turn out to vote. Others may not trust the uneducated and other underrepresented segments of the public because of their belief in the intrinsic value of elite decision-making.[3]

There are many others, however, who do see a substantial benefit to higher voter turnout. V.O. Key, a prominent political scientist, argues: "The blunt truth is that politicians and officials are under no compulsion to pay much heed to classes and groups of citizens that do not vote."[4] The implication is that those not voting will be underrepresented and suffer accordingly. Others make a persuasive case that individuals benefit psychologically by participating in politics.[5] Moreover, it is widely recognized that unequal participation translates into unequal representation and "unequal influence."[6] This in turn has been found to have an effect on policy outcomes at the local,[7] state,[8] and national[9] levels of government. Last, the lack of participation has implications for democratic legitimacy with lower participation, in the aggregate, compromising political support.[10]

This research is in good company when it advocates for a more engaged citizenry. This is hardly an extreme position. Indeed, the opposition to this point of view is more obviously rebellious. Yet can one assume that more viable third parties will prompt more citizen involvement in politics? The most easily measureable indicator of citizen participation is voter turnout. Previous research on turnout suggests a major factor explaining variation is "mobilization" or the extent to which groups, or elites, seek to rally individuals to show themselves at the polls.[11] Furthermore, studies argue this is exactly what political parties can be expected to do. Prominent researchers have found that among the important explanations for the decline in voter turnout witnessed in the United States in the 1970s and 1980s was the lack of voter mobilization by political parties.[12]

Figure 5.1 displays data representing the average level of third party voting and voter turnout, by states, in the eight most recent presidential elections.

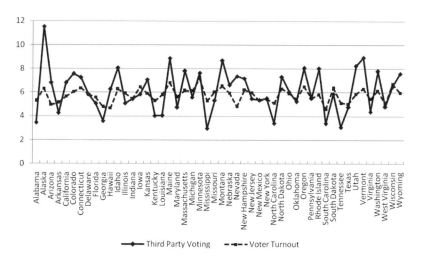

Figure 5.1 Third party voting in presidential elections and voter turnout by state: 1980–2008.

Note: The aggregate correlation between the two lines is $r = .65$; $p < .01$; $n = 50$ and the disaggregated correlation is $r = .11$; $p < .05$; $n = 400$.

Voter turnout is divided by ten so that the line representing this dynamic will appear congruent with third party voting in the Figure. Reading across the horizontal line corresponding with 8 percent third party voting, one can count eight states that supported third party presidential candidates at this level or higher. The states are Alaska, Idaho, Maine, Montana, Oregon, Rhode Island, Utah, and Vermont. Notably, only two of the eight states had a voter turnout rate lower than 60 percent (Rhode Island and Utah), the eight states had an average voter turnout rate of 62.9 percent, and none of the eight states had a voter turnout rate below 58.2 percent. Also interesting, beyond region, the states would not seem to have much in common. Five of the eight states are from the West—but there is a liberal Western state (Oregon) and conservative Western states (Idaho and Utah). The remaining three states are from New England and represent two of the country's most liberal states (Rhode Island and Vermont) and a relatively conservative New England state (Maine).[13] It would seem that higher third party voting and higher voter turnout is centered in New England and the far West, but consistent with both liberal and conservative state ideologies.

The type of correlation analysis presented in Figure 5.1 does not explain a causal relationship between third party voting and voter turnout. Indeed, one might imagine that something about the culture of Western and New England states, although they are notably distinct, might be causing both higher third party voting and voter turnout. To gain more leverage on the "true" relationship between third party voting and voter turnout it is necessary to conduct additional tests.

More Preliminary Tests

Anecdotally, one can note that when the country moved from a one-party dominant system, during the "era of good feeling" (1817–25), which ended with the hotly contested presidential election of 1824, to an era of meaningful two-party competition that voter turnout went from 26.9 (1824) percent to 57.6 percent (1828). The 1824 election saw the House of Representatives picking the president because the Electoral College could not produce a candidate with majority support. The country was divided, a new political party was born (the Whigs), and voter turnout increased by over 100 percent!

Considering a second anecdote, there has been only one presidential election in the history of the United States that witnessed something akin to multi-party democracy and meaningful multi-party electoral competition. This was the election of 1860, the last election won by a third party presidential candidate, Abraham Lincoln. When one compares voter turnout immediately prior to and after the election of 1860 to voter turnout in the election of 1860, a notable design is discernable. The average voter turnout rate in the elections of 1852 and 1856 was 74 percent, voter turnout in 1860 was 81 percent, and the average turnout in 1864 and 1868 was again

74 percent. The one instance of multi-party democracy in the United States is associated with about a 7 percent increase in voter turnout in the presidential election.

The historical anecdotes are interesting but the focus throughout this book has been the modern era. Because the normative concern is viable third parties in the 21st century, the dominant mode of inquiry has been to examine the modern electoral context. As noted previously, extending the empirical analyses to earlier eras runs the risk of mixing data representing unique historical conditions with modern data in a way that can cause faulty inferences for the contemporary period. Unfortunately, the number of *viable* third party candidates in recent years is limited. Yet, it simply does not make sense to study third party voting when the third electoral option is not moderately feasible. There is no reason to expect non-viable third party candidates to comport with systematic change in citizen participation rates. Moving forward, only elections that had reasonably viable third party candidates running, in the post World War II era, will be considered in the voter turnout tests.

Considering this, there are four presidential elections that one can reasonably consider; specifically the elections of 1968, 1980, 1992, and 1996. The 1968 presidential campaign saw George Wallace, the American Independent Party candidate, winning Electoral College votes, the last third party candidate to do so. Moreover, Wallace wins 13.5 percent of the popular vote. Second, there was the independent candidacy of John Anderson from Ohio in 1980. Anderson receives 6.6 percent of the popular vote, a level of support that is not particularly promising, but the 1980 election is included because Anderson received considerable media attention that year. As late as September 1980, he was included in a presidential debate with the major party candidates by the League of Women Voters.[14] Third, the 1992 presidential election found Ross Perot shocking the two-party establishment by polling neck-and-neck with the major party candidates as late as June 1992.[15] Perot ends up with 18.9 percent of the popular vote, but no Electoral College support as he does not win any of the 50 states. Last, there is the 1996 election when Perot received 8.4 percent of the votes cast. The novelty of the Perot candidacy had worn off which makes this election less relevant in terms of viability, but if one adds votes received by other third party presidential candidates in 1996, the third party presidential vote total climbs to over 10 percent of all votes cast.

The initial turnout analysis, presented below, includes all four instances of third party presidential candidates receiving a reasonable level of support. When this research moves to test the relationship between third party voting and voter turnout in a regression analysis, the Wallace election is dropped from consideration. The 1968 election is interesting, but when one moves to test alternative considerations that might affect voter turnout in today's highly competitive electoral climate, the 1968 election is not helpful. Specifically, Wallace was only popular in Southern states and these states in 1968 were outliers in terms of their electoral conditions. Again, it does not make sense to mix data from an earlier era representing an electoral climate that no longer exists with data from the modern era when the normative concern is the future. In all the tests that follow, the American state is the unit of analysis. The test, which uses all four instances when third party presidential candidates had some success, considers 50 individual state values but averages them for presentation in Table 5.1.

In order to test the significance of viable third party presidential candidates, and then gubernatorial candidates, on voter turnout the following equation is used:

$$(TO_t - TO_{t-1}) - (TO_{t+1} - TO_t)$$

TO_t equals voter turnout when a viable third party candidate is running; TO_{t-1} equals voter turnout in the election prior to the viable third party running; and TO_{t+1} equals voter turnout in the election after the viable third party was running. Because Ross Perot ran in back to back elections in 1992 and 1996, the equation above is modified to account for the possibility that what really matters is voter turnout before and after the viable third party run is complete and there is no longer a viable third party candidate on the ballot. In this instance the equation equals:

$$(_{AVG} TO_{tn} - TO_{t-1}) - (TO_{t+1} - {_{AVG}} TO_{tn}).$$

Where $_{AVG} TO_{tn}$ is the average voter turnout for the consecutive elections that had a viable third party candidate running.

Table 5.1 exhibits the results of this test representing a quasi-experimental design with a pretest, interaction, and post-test. Looking first at the 1968 election, voter turnout was about the same as it had been in the 1964 election, but was 5.5 percent higher than turnout in 1972. The 1960s were a time of decreasing voter turnout nationwide—and it appears that the Wallace

Table 5.1 Viable Third Party Presidential Candidates and Voter Turnout: 50 State Averages

Year	Candidate	Turnout$_{t-1}$	Turnout$_t$	Turnout$_{t+1}$	$(TO_t - TO_{t-1}) -$ $(TO_{t+1} - TO_t)$*
1968	Wallace	62.1	61.8	56.3	5.2
1980	Anderson	55.1	54.8	56.7	−2.3
1992–96	Perot	54.7	56.8	55.8	3.2
1992	Perot	54.7	60.3	53.4	12.5
	Totals	56.65	58.42	55.55	4.64

* Three out of four cases witnessed a positive association between viable third party presidential candidates and voter turnout. Column values may be affected by rounding.

candidacy was associated with an interruption of the downward spiral, albeit short lived. Considering the 1980 election, one can note turnout was actually lower than it had been in either 1976 or 1984 campaigns, but not appreciably so. This had been somewhat anticipated. Anderson's level of support was not likely sufficient to produce a positive relationship between voting for a non-major party presidential candidate and voter turnout. Next, examining the combined 1992 and 1996 elections, voter turnout was higher. The test returns a positive value and finds voter turnout slightly higher in 1992–96 than in either the presidential election immediately previous or subsequent to these two election cycles. The substantive difference, however, is not dramatic. Last, when one looks at only the 1992 election, the change in voter turnout associated with Ross Perot's first run, representing the election that arguably witnessed the "most" viable third party candidate, there is a very noticeable difference. Voter turnout in 1992 was about 6 percent higher than it had been in the previous and succeeding presidential elections.

The four tests of the relationship between voter turnout and viable third party presidential candidates in the modern era are not overwhelmingly conclusive. However, the totals exhibited in the last row of Table 5.1 suggest that at minimum viable third party candidates are not disengaging the public and are probably enhancing turnout levels, on average. It is possible to go a step further with this analysis and look at viable third party candidates in governor races. Here, it is possible to obtain a larger sample so that one can have more confidence in the test results. In considering governor's races, the calculation is made each instance in the post-World War II era when a third party gubernatorial candidate received at least 10 percent of the vote. The only exceptions are the Illinois and Texas gubernatorial elections in 2006, the Louisiana gubernatorial election in 2007, and the Vermont gubernatorial election in 2008. These elections were not included because the voter turnout for their subsequent elections was unavailable at the time the data were collected for this research.

Using the guidelines spelled out above, there are 35 cases or instances when it is possible to test the relationship between voter turnout and viable third party candidates in governor races. Table 5.2 exhibits the results. Nineteen of the 35 cases produce a positive difference and the "Total" difference representing the average values of each of the columns suggests viable third party candidates are, on average, associated with greater voter turnout. The bivariate correlation between third party voting percentages (not shown in the table) and the values presented in the fourth column is positive but not statistically significant ($r = .11$; n = 35).

A closer examination of the data presented in Table 5.2, however, reveals that one state is compromising a more positive finding. The state of Maine produces six of the 35 cases shown and in each instance viable third party candidates are not associated positively with voter turnout. If data from Maine is removed from the analysis, now 19 of 29 (66 percent) of the cases produce

Table 5.2 Viable Third Party Gubernatorial Candidates and Voter Turnout

Year	State	$Turnout_{t-1}$	Turnout	$Turnout_{t+1}$	$(_{AVG}TO_{tn} - TO_{t-1}) - (TO_{t+1} - _{AVG}TO_{tn})$
1952	Maine	49.7	43.1	52.9	-16.4
1956	Utah	84.1	85.4	79.3	7.5
1962	Tennessee	21.9	29.7	29.7	7.8
1965	Virginia	17.0	23.3	35.5	-6.0
1966	Idaho	68.6	74.9	58.6	22.5
1972	New Hampshire	67.7	62.0	59.3	-3.0
1974	Maine	54.1	50.4	55.5	-8.8
1974	Nevada	48.5	43.3	45.2	-7.0
1978	Alaska	45.1	57.9	49.6	21.1
1978	Maine	51.0	49.8	55.5	-6.9
1982	Alaska	54.0	61.5	49.6	19.4
1982	Hawaii	46.6	43.1	43.1	-3.5
1986	Arizona	34.4	35.3	39.0	-2.8
1986	Maine	55.5	49.0	56.5	-14.0
1986	Vermont	44.6	49.7	50.1	4.7
1988	Utah	61.6	61.2	47.7	13.0
1990	Alaska	49.6	51.5	51.0	2.4
1990	Connecticut	40.1	45.3	39.3	11.2
1990	New York	31.8	29.5	37.5	-10.3
1990	Oregon	53.2	52.1	52.1	-1.1
1992	Utah	60.5	61.8	47.7	15.4
1994	Alaska	51.3	51.6	51.0	0.9
1994	Connecticut	45.0	45.6	39.3	6.9
1994	Hawaii	41.7	41.8	44.8	-2.9
1994	Maine	56.5	52.9	50.1	-0.9
1994	New Mexico	38.2	39.1	38.8	1.2
1994	Oklahoma	39.4	41.3	34.7	8.5
1994	Pennsylvania	33.5	38.8	37.3	6.8
1998	Alaska	51.2	52.0	51.0	1.8
1998	Maine	54.9	50.8	50.1	-3.4
1998	Minnesota	55.2	63.6	60.5	11.6
1998	Pennsylvania	38.8	32.5	37.3	-11.1
2002	Minnesota	62.3	64.9	60.5	7.0
2002	New York	33.5	31.4	30.3	-1.0
2002	Oklahoma	34.7	39.6	34.3	10.2
	Total	47.87	48.73	47.28	2.31

a positive difference in voter turnout. The average difference found in the "Total" row, the last Column, climbs from 2.31 to 4.52. Moreover, there is now a positive and statistically significant association between the level of third party voting and the values in Column 4 ($r = .36$; $p < .05$ one-tailed test; n = 29). It seems Maine's experience with third parties differs from what other states encounter. In particular, gubernatorial candidates have fared very well and this point deserves additional attention by future research.

Next, this research moves to test the relationship between third party voting and voter turnout in a statistical model that controls for a host of other considerations that previous research suggests will determine variation in state-level voter turnout rates. An elaboration of the research design for this particular test is provided below. This will be followed by the elaboration of a test which seeks to measure the relationship between third party voting in modern presidential elections and an indicator of the density of citizen-interest groups in the American states.

The Research Design

Any research seeking to test variables that influence variation in voter turnout rates will be confronted with an overabundance of existing research to build on.[16] There are models that use the individual voter as the unit of analysis, aggregate models that test cross-national variance in voter turnout, and others that examine state-by-state variance in the United States. Single variables such as education or the closeness of elections have been responsible for dozens of articles.[17] There will be no attempt, here, to improve on the measurement of either education or the closeness of election or to improve on the model specification decisions made by others. Instead, this research will simply account for considerations that others argue are important while attempting to hone in on whether the presence of viable third party candidates is associated with greater voter turnout in the American states. Then, the research turns to the issue of citizen-interest group density.

Third Party Voting and Voter Turnout

The dependent variable in this test will be state-level voter turnout when a viable third party presidential candidate is on the ballot. As noted earlier, the analysis is limited to the modern era. Specifically, the research tests the relationship between the level of third party voting in each American state and state-level voter turnout in the 1980, 1992, and 1996 presidential elections.[18] This provides a test of the relationship using a sample of 150 elections; 50 states and three presidential election cycles.

The key explanatory variable will be the level of non-major party voting in each state. Figure 5.2 displays state variation on this variable averaged over the three presidential elections. In the regression analysis the data will be disaggregated. One can notice that many of the states at the top of the list are the same states that had high third party voting and voter turnout in the time period 1980–2008, as exhibited in Figure 5.1. Specifically, Alaska, Maine, Vermont, Rhode Island, and Montana have the highest levels of non-major party voting for president in the three election cycles now being considered. Notably, the bottom ten states are all from the old South where traditional culture has often worked against political innovation and progressive ideals.[19]

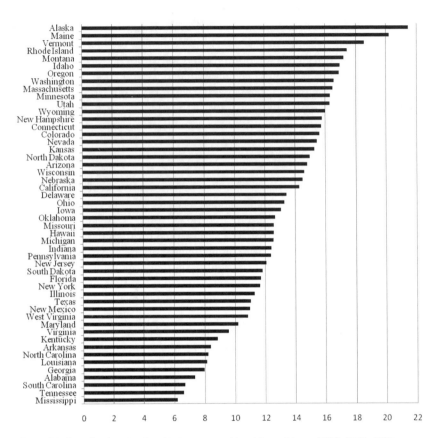

Figure 5.2 State level voting for third party presidential candidates: 1980, 1992, 1996 (The Key Explanatory Variable).

Considering all 150 state elections, the minimum value of 2.3 percent third party voting occurs in South Carolina in 1980 and the maximum value of 30.8 percent occurs in Maine in 1992. The average value in the 50 states over the three election cycles is 13.1 percent with a standard deviation of 6.7 percent.

The turnout model controls for six additional considerations that might be expected to influence variation in voter turnout in the American states. First, the closeness of the election between the Democratic and Republican candidate in the state is taken into account. The primary thesis has been that close elections ought to spur greater voter turnout because the probability that one's vote matters will increase.[20] Others suggest that it is not the closeness of the election, but rather increased voter mobilization efforts that occur when an election is close.[21] In any event, the hypothesis here is that when the absolute value of the difference in the vote percentage received by Democrats and

Republicans grows, there will be an associated decrease in voter turnout. A negative coefficient is expected.

Second, the research controls for state educational achievement.[22] Researchers contest this issue hotly. Some suggesting it is not education per se, but instead information that is the causal agent.[23] What is not debated is that models of voter turnout, whether at an individual level or an aggregate level,[24] must in some way account for "education." In this research, the percentage of a state's citizens that hold a college degree is employed. The anticipation is that this will be positively associated with voter turnout, all else being equal. Third, the research controls for variance in the difficulty of voter registration requirements in the American states.[25] In particular, this research uses the number of days prior to an election that a citizen must get registered to vote as a proxy for state variation in registration difficulty. States such as North Dakota, which does not require voter registration, and Maine and Minnesota, which allow same day registration, are scored "0" and the expectation is that large values on this variable will be associated with lower voter turnout.

The fourth consideration is the relationship between economic adversity and voter turnout. Citing classic literature, one point of view is that economic limitations will increase voter turnout because people will blame the government for their economic woes and will seek to punish incumbent office holders.[26] Others, however, note that the poor are often preoccupied with survival and may not have the time or opportunity to vote.[27] Given countervailing expectations, this research employs an interactive measurement of economic duress. Specifically, each state's unemployment level, poverty level, and the interaction of unemployment and poverty (Unemployment * Poverty) are entered into the regression equation. Given the analysis is limited to modern times and the American states, the expectation is that both unemployment and poverty will be mobilizing agents prompting higher levels of voter turnout. However, their interaction ought to be associated with lower levels of turnout. The interaction of the two economic variables arguably captures something akin to severe economic hardship, the type of economic adversity that others have theorized may depress voter turnout.

The fifth and sixth considerations are measures that have been used in previous chapters, although with some countervailing expectations. It was previously found that when one of the two major political parties was missing from the ballot, this prompted greater third party voting. The expectation in this instance is that the lack of major party competition will be associated with lower voter turnout producing a negative coefficient in the regression analysis. The sixth consideration is "one-party dominance" or the extent to which the politics of a state, specifically a state lower chamber, is dominated by a single major party. In the earlier chapters it was found that this variable was associated with less third party voting. The anticipation here is the same. One-party dominance and its associated lack of electoral competition ought to be linked to lower state-level voter turnout rates.

Another Test of the Relationship between Third Party Voting and Civic Engagement

Virginia Gray and David Lowery, two prominent scholars of American state government, developed a measure of the frequency of active citizen-interest groups in the United States.[28] Their annual measure of the number of active citizen groups in each state has no missing values after 1990 and extends through 1999. The data collection ceased after 1999 because of a lack of resources.[29] Given this limitation, it is still possible to test the relationship between third party voting in the American states and the frequency of citizen-interest groups in three presidential election cycles (1992, 1996, and 2000), provided one allows the use of the 1999 citizen group values for the 2000 presidential election. To be clear, the measure of active citizen-interest groups is intended to serve as a surrogate for civic engagement.

One can argue that this test of third party voting and participation is compromised by only 150 data points and data that are arrayed across states in continuous presidential election cycles. This reality prompts the use of a generalized least squares regression technique, which accounts for data clustered in this manner. The modeling choice is explained in more detail in the Appendix to this chapter. Moreover, it is important to control for the size of each state but, more specifically, each state's economy. To account for this, Gray and Lowery divide the actual number of citizen groups by Gross State Product (GSP), in millions, to obtain something akin to "citizen-interest group density" in the states. The decision to divide the frequency of groups by GSP is motivated by the assumption that higher levels of economic activity will be associated with more interest group action. This calculation controls for the possibility that a state might have fewer interest groups but even less overall economic activity. For instance, Wyoming in 1992 had fewer active groups than some other states but proportionately had an even smaller GSP. Hence, Wyoming obtains the highest value on what is the dependent variable in this test.

The calculation described above was performed independently for this research. In the time period analyzed, the state (and year) with the lowest level of citizen interest group density is Virginia in 2000 (3.56×10^{-4}) and the case with the highest level of interest group density is Wyoming in 1992 (.011). Higher values, arguably, represent a relatively higher level of interest group membership and activity in the state. In this test of the relationship between third party voting and civic engagement, the research, again, controls for the percentage of state citizens that are college graduates. The abbreviated statistical model also includes GSP, which ought to be negatively associated with interest group density. Because GSP is part of the dependent variable (as the denominator), states with more economic activity (higher GSP) are obtaining relatively lower values on the measure of civic engagement. Hence, greater GSP ought to be associated with lower values on the dependent variable. This control variable can be expected to account for considerable variation in the dependent variable providing a more meaningful test of the other considerations.

Results

Table 5.3 presents the results of the test of third party voting and voter turnout in the three most recent presidential elections that included a reasonable third party option on the ballot. The check for association is overwhelmingly conclusive. The coefficient is seven times the standard error, suggesting a very robust relationship between the two concerns. The coefficient value of .49 suggests that a 1 percentage increase in third party voting is associated with nearly a half percentage increase in voter turnout, all else being equal. Put differently, a 10 percent increase in third party voting is linked to about a 4.9 percent increase in voter turnout, on average, and this is the case after controlling for several other considerations.

The only control variable that does not perform as hypothesized is the indicator of the Democratic–Republican vote gap. In this instance, the test returns a statistically significant coefficient in the direction opposite of what had been hypothesized. This variable has produced countervailing findings in past research, so perhaps after controlling for third party voting it should not be surprising that the two major party vote gap does not perform as anticipated.[30] The education variable performs as expected: a 1 percentage point increase in a state's population that has a college degree is associated with over

Table 5.3 State Level Voter Turnout when a "Viable" Third Party Presidential Candidate is Running: 1980, 1992, 1996

Model: Ordinary Least Squares Regression—See the Appendix for details.

	Exp. Sign	Coefficient (standard error)
Key Explanatory Variable		
Third Party Voting	+	.49 (.07)***
Control Variables		
DEM–REP Vote Gap	–	7.72 (4.65)*-
College Educated Population	+	.18 (.08)**
Registration Difficulty	–	-.38 (.04)***
Unemployment	+	3.13 (.74)***
Poverty	+	1.09 (.43)**
Unemployment* Poverty	–	-.16 (.06)**
Majority Party Missing	–	-93 (2.41)
One-Party Dominance	–	-2.84 (1.89)ᵗ
Constant		34.23 (5.88)***
R²		.66
n		150

*** $p < .001$; ** $p < .01$; * $p < .05$; ᵗ $p < .10$ (one-tailed tests)
– Significant in the direction opposite of what had been hypothesized

Table 5.4 State Level Interest Group Density and Third Party Voting: 1992, 1996, 2000

Model: Random-effects Generalized Least Squares Regression

	Exp. Sign	Coefficient (standard error)
Key Explanatory Variable		
Third Party Voting	+	6.18×10^{-5} (1.73×10^{-5})***
Control Variables		
College Educated Population	+	6.22×10^{-5} (3.30×10^{-5})*
Gross State Product	−	-2.28×10^{-9} (9.90×10^{-10})**
Constant		1.72×10^{-4} (8.88×10^{-4})
R^2 – overall		.22
n		150

*** $p < .001$; ** $p < .01$; * $p < .05$ (one-tailed tests)

a 7.7 percent increase in voter turnout, on average. The economic variables also perform as expected: state unemployment and poverty are associated with greater voter turnout, and their interaction with less. The variable representing the extent to which major party candidates are missing from the ballot in each state does produce a negative coefficient, as anticipated, but this is not a statistically significant consideration. Last, one-party dominance is marginally associated with lower voter turnout as projected.

Table 5.4 presents the results of the test seeking to uncover a relationship between third party voting and an alternative indicator of civic engagement— citizen-interest group density. This model run is not intended to uncover all there is to know about the relationship between third party activity and interest groups. Rather the motivation is to simply provide an auxiliary check on the relationship between third parties and civic engagement uncovered in the turnout model. Given this limited purpose, the results obtained are encouraging. Because the number of groups in each state is divided by GSP, the coefficients produced by the test are quite small and difficult to interpret.[31] What is clear, however, is that there is a strong statistically significant relationship between third party voting and citizen interest group density. This is the case after controlling for an indicator of state educational attainment and GSP. Both control variables are statistically linked to interest group density in the manner hypothesized. The results of this auxiliary test complement the positive relationship uncovered between third party voting and voter turnout.

Conclusion

This research has shown that third party voting is easily associated with greater citizen participation in elections, on average. It is not the case that viable third party candidates will always spike voter turnout levels, as there are many different considerations that can and do affect voter turnout rates. However, when one looks beyond individual instances and analyzes the question using average values across the modern era, the unmistakable conclusion is drawn that viable third party candidates are a boon to voter turnout levels. There is also a state-level correlation between third party voting and interest group activity in the American states.

It now seems there is an additional consequence to two-party dominance. It had been shown in Chapter 4 that landmark productivity was enhanced by the presence of third parties in Congress. Now, it appears that third parties can also propel increased civic engagement. The analyses in this chapter suggest viable third party candidates are associated with aggregate state-level differences in citizen participation rates. It would seem some people are not impressed with the two-major party options provided in most American elections.

In sum, it is not the case that two-party dominance occurs without consequences. George Wallace, in 1968, suggested there is not "a dime's worth of difference" between Democrats and Republicans. This is likely an overstatement. However, it would now appear that when confronted with third electoral options, on average, people are sufficiently impressed with the added choice to be more likely to participate in elections. Viable minor party electoral competition and a more engaged citizenry seem to go hand-in-hand.

Appendix: Model Specifications

In Table 5.3 the estimates are obtained using an Ordinary Least Squares Regression. The data points represent different time periods; however, this is not a true time series specification because the time periods are interrupted. Moreover, a Breusch–Pagan/Cook–Weisberg test for heteroskedasticity suggests that one can to a certain extent reject the null hypothesis of constant variance ($Chi^2 = 3.63$; $p < .06$). Coefficients represent the effect a one-unit increase in an independent variable has on the percentage of the voting-age population that turnout.

In Table 5.4 the estimates are obtained by means of a cross-sectional time-series random effects regression model. Specifically, the research uses the Generalized Least Squares estimator to produce a matrix weighted average of the between and within results. The model applies to data sets where the number of cross-sections is larger than the number of time points. This model provides estimates that are not affected by heteroskedasticity or autocorrelation problems common to the estimation of cross-sectional longitudinal data.[32] The dependent variable is the number of active citizen groups in the state divided by the Gross State Product in millions. Coefficients represent the effect a one-unit increase in an independent variable on the number of citizen interest groups/GSP.

Chapter 6

How to Make Third Parties Viable Once More?

Central to the debate over third parties in the United States is the question of the desirability of minor party involvement in the American political system. Critics charge that disrupting a two-party system may induce government instability and make automatic governing majorities less likely, risking decreased accountability to the public.[1] Advocates of electoral reform, for their part, champion minor parties as a causeway to more inclusive representation[2] and as a fertile source of innovative public policy prescriptions.[3] It is also argued that viable third party candidates allow for legitimate expression of public dissent.[4] What has often been missing from these largely theoretical debates is an attempt to learn the whole truth about what is preventing third party competition in the United States along with efforts to empirically test the consequences of two-party dominance.

This research has endeavored to show the truth and consequences regarding the lack of third party representation in the United States. It should be clear now that plurality rule elections and single-member districts are the most important impediment to sustained third party electoral success in the United States. The secret ballot also played a role in diminishing the likelihood of successful third parties, but not so much because of restricted ballot access. Instead, third party operatives are no longer given the same opportunity to out-hustle their major party counterparts. The research has also uncovered that two-party dominance comes with real-world consequences. Specifically, two dominant political parties in Congress, without third party protection, can compromise legislative productivity. When third party success was more commonplace, the legislative process benefited. In the late 19th century, the Progressive era, and to some extent the New Deal era, viable third parties worked to either attenuate or exacerbate conflict, as necessary, to cause landmark legislative accomplishment. Still more, this research has uncovered evidence of a relationship between third party electoral involvement and increased civic engagement in the form of voting, and also a relationship with citizen-interest group density.

It is not the case anymore that the benefits of third parties are only theoretical. Rigorous case study analysis and econometric modeling has uncovered empirical/systematic evidence of the value of viable third parties in the United States. Previous research acknowledged, perhaps too readily, the practical and political infeasibility of changing the existing single-member districts with plurality rule (SMD-PR) electoral arrangements responsible for two-party dominance in the United States.[5] The alleged improbability of reform has led scholars to presume third party voting for legislative seats in the United States to be unworthy of further investigation. But, earlier historical eras did witness more third party success under the same SMD-PR election laws that exist today[6] and countries with similar SMD-PR constraints, such as the United Kingdom and Canada, have viable minor party options. Consequently, the SMD-PR election format is not a sufficient condition to block meaningful third party representation in legislatures.

Given this reality, the objective of this remaining chapter is to suggest changes that could and would prompt more viable third parties in the United States. Particularly important, these changes do not require a return back to party-sponsored ballots, are reasonably modest, would not produce a full blown multi-party system, and do not require constitutional change.

Changes that would Prompt More Viable Third Political Parties

The arguments made in Chapter 1 in opposition to third parties largely come from those who fear a pure multi-party democratic system is too complicated and unstable. Moreover, there is concern that geographic representation would be compromised if the whole country consisted of a single electoral constituency. These fears may be more a product of the unknown, or fear of things foreign, than they are a realistic assessment of what a proportional representation system would look like in the United States. But let us assume that the arguments have merit, that a full-blown or purely proportional system is somehow problematic. Then, what about the myriad of electoral options that exist which would not prompt multi-party democracy, but would encourage third parties nonetheless? There are multiple ways to encourage viable third electoral options other than the adoption of proportional representation elections.

Duverger's Law suggests both single-member districts and plurality rule are required to squash third party success. Altering one but not the other can break two-party dominance without unleashing electoral success for numerous small political parties with limited agendas. For instance, it would be possible to simply disrupt single-member districts. It was shown in the conclusion to Chapter 3 that when the state of Illinois had multi-member districts, third parties fared better but two-dominant political parties were still the norm. A second option would be to invoke a majority rule in legislative elections instead of the plurality rule so routinely used today. Australia, Ireland, Mexico, and other countries have used majority rule for legislative elections and, as a consequence, these countries have more experience with viable third parties but largely remain two-party dominant systems.[7]

A third possible change would be to increase the size of the national legislature. This would decrease the size of constituencies providing better geographic representation in Congress—a major concern of those who support the status quo of no change. Third parties, representing more extreme positions, would fare better in smaller constituencies that lean either left or right ideologically. The median voter may be closer to the issue positions of the third party and the reduced size of the political turf would allow third party candidates an opportunity to out battle their major party opponents. This consideration is almost certainly the best explanation for why the United Kingdom has viable third parties in the House of Commons while maintaining SMD-PR elections.

Each of the three reform options just offered will be discussed in more detail below. It is important to keep in mind as one considers these possibilities what the United States Constitution says about elections to Congress. Article 1, Section 4 states "The Times, Places and manner of holding Elections for Senators and Representatives, shall be prescribed in each State by the Legislature thereof." The Constitution does not forbid multi-member districts and majority rule and many states have used each. In the early years of the Republic, members of the House of Representatives were almost exclusively elected at-large or in multi-member districts. The term "at-large" suggests members are elected in mass, in a single-constituency, without geographic districts. Congress, and more specifically Whigs and Democrats, got into the act in 1842, mandating that representatives be elected in single-member districts. Yet even after this law passed, several states simply ignored the directive.[8] Subsequently, several new laws and court decisions clouded the issue until the 90th Congress (1967–68) wrote a new law, Public Law 90–196, which once again established single-member districts for the House of Representatives. Undoing this law may be at the heart of meaningful reform which would allow for viable third parties to return to Congress.

There is no constitutional or statutory restriction on the use of majority rule or the specific type of elections used by states to elect members of their state legislature or local political offices. Indeed, there is tremendous variation in the manner in which states conduct elections. It was shown in Chapter 2 that states have unique primary election laws, unique ballot access procedures, and unique laws regarding the practice of fusion candidates. Moreover, it was shown in Chapter 3 that states, particularly Florida and Maryland, can and do change election procedures when prompted to do so by public awareness and discontent with the restrictive status quo.

Multi-Member Districts

The notion of multi-member districts should not be foreign to American voters. The state of Illinois had multi-member districts for state legislators as recently as the late 1970s. Moreover, United State's senators are elected in a type of multi-member district—two senators from each state. However, this does not support third parties because the two members elected from the same constituency are elected in separate elections. In order for multi-member districts to have the effect of producing viable third parties, the members need to be selected in a single election. If the two United States senators from each state were elected at the same time with the top two vote-getters securing a seat, this would change the probability of electing third party members to the United States Senate. A third party's best chance would likely occur in a state with one dominant major party. The dominant party would receive the most votes and would always have representation, but a third party in these instances might finish second on occasion. If a state elects only one member at a time, the dominant party wins all the time.

It is also common in the United States to use true multi-member districts for local offices. It is not surprising that recent Green Party victories in local elections often occur in multi-member districts or at-large elections. For instance, the city of Oshkosh, Wisconsin elects the city's Common Council at-large. In 2007, a Green Party candidate won a seat by finishing with the third highest vote total in a race with seven candidates. In the 2010 Oshkosh city election, another Green Party candidate won a seat on the Common Council by finishing fourth. The city of Minneapolis, Minnesota uses a form of preferential voting, similar to that used to elect members of the Australian House of Representatives, to elect members to the Parks and Recreation Board and a Green Party member recently won an election to the Board by finishing second. Still more, Green Party members were recently elected to the Portland, Maine City Council and the New London, Connecticut City Council. Both cities use at-large elections which allow for more than one winner.[9]

It is not the case that multi-member districts and placing the top two, three, or four vote-getters into a legislative body is unheard of in the United States. It is done in cities and counties throughout the country. This type of election could be used for elections to state legislatures, or the United States Congress if anyone cared enough and possessed sufficient resources to mount a grass-roots effort to undo P.L. 90–196, which mandates single-member districts for United States House seats. In the process, the movement might expose the fallacy that the Democratic and Republican Parties offer all the electoral choice required for an engaged citizenry and an effective legislative process. There would be opposition to be sure, but even the most sensible counter arguments to multi-member districts are far from infallible.

Critiques of this type of change would likely argue that two-member districts for state legislatures and Congress would require larger constituencies. If there are only "X" number of seats in the legislature and a change is made to elect two candidates from each electoral district, the number of districts would need to be reduced by "X/2." The number of electoral districts would need to be cut in half in order to preserve the current size of the legislature. Continuing with the critique, opponents of change might argue, if there were both a rich and a poor part to the new larger district, the top two vote-getters might both come from the rich part of the district and so leave the poor part without the representation which it previously enjoyed.

This seemingly good argument is flawed. The assumption is made that the number of seats in a legislature needs to remain constant. If the number of seats in the legislature increased to "2X," the argument falls apart, and geographic representation would actually be improved. If one would simply double the size of the legislature, the same district lines could be used and geographic representation would improve. The change would produce increased geographic representation, not reduced representation, and the poorest part of town would have a better chance of seating a member from their area.

A further discussion of increasing the number of representatives in legislatures will be offered below. Suffice it to say for now that creating multi-member districts is not as radical as it might seem. Again, we frequently use multi-member districts in local elections. This change would not require a constitutional amendment, and once the national law was changed, the reform could be implemented piecemeal with some states experimenting with multi-member districts for United States House seats while other states waited. After seeing that the change, back to the way members of the House of Representatives were selected prior to 1842, does not rock the foundation of democracy, more states might make the decision to adopt.

Majority Rule Elections

This type of voting is also not foreign to the United States. Majority rule is used to adopt legislation in Congress and state legislatures and is commonly used in meetings of a variety of types. Majority rule is used in some Southern state major-party primaries; majority rule is used in the state of Louisiana elections; and majority rule is used to select members to the United States Congress from the state of Georgia. Majority rule is so common that it is difficult to imagine how the people of the Untied States have come to embrace plurality rule. When asking undergraduate political science majors about election law in the United States, it is not uncommon to learn that many assume the country uses majority rule. The best explanation for the widespread acceptance of plurality rule would seem to be ignorance. Perhaps a cultural or political hegemony argument could be made. The public accepts plurality rule as appropriate because they do not know there are alternatives and because they have been socialized to accept the condition, or state of affairs, that currently exists.

Imagine sitting in a meeting where three alternative courses of action are being considered. The chair of the meeting suggests a vote and proclaims that whatever option gets the most votes will win straightaway. Someone present will almost certainly object, suggesting a second round of voting once the least favored option is determined and eliminated from consideration. Assuming the least favorite option had some support, those who backed this choice will have considerable sway in the next round of voting. They may throw all of their votes to the second favorite option creating majority support for this course of action. Alternatively, they may side with the plurality winner from the first round and cause that option to be overwhelmingly accepted. In either instance, supporters of the least favorite option lost their preferred option, but were empowered by the opportunity to make a difference in the second round of voting.

The same thing happens around the world in countries that use majority rule elections. The third party may be the least favorite option, but the party's supporters will often have some say in who does win a runoff election. This level of influence encourages third parties and provides them with a reason to stick around from one election cycle to the next. The third parties may not win actual seats in the legislature, but they are in a position where the major political parties cannot take them for granted or ignore them completely. They may need the third party's support in present or future runoff elections. Indeed, given this scenario, one might even imagine the major political parties being willing to respectfully consider third party ideas or issue positions!

Again, this type of reform is hardly radical. A couple of states already use majority rule. Unfortunately, both Louisiana and Georgia have other electoral arrangements that work to thwart third party electoral achievement. Louisiana uses non-partisan ballots that serve to confuse everyone about who they are voting for.[10] Georgia has a political culture that is reluctant to embrace anything different,[11] and has some of the most restrictive third party ballot access laws in the country.

The best argument critics of majority rule will likely be able to muster is that it causes the need for an additional round of costly elections to decide the winner. This argument is incomplete for at least two reasons. First, the costs associated with the status quo of two-party dominance are not considered. This research has uncovered major costs in the form of gridlock in the legislative process and an unenthused electorate. Both of these costs are difficult to quantify, but to assume the dollars needed to hold a second round of elections would be greater than the benefit derived from viable third parties could be a mistake. Second, we already have a myriad of elections being held around the country, in the different states, all the time.[12] Meaningful reform might eliminate, consolidate, and reduce the number of elections currently being held.[13] It is not at all unreasonable to assume that it would be possible to have majority rule runoff elections and actually reduce the total number of elections, if rational reformers would take change seriously.

Increasing the Size of Congress

The last change considered is one that others claim is important for different reasons. Brian Frederick has argued for increasing the size of the national legislature, not to promote third parties but to simply improve representation and bring it closer to home.[14] His case is that broader more inclusive representation improves public perceptions of government, which causes greater public approval and government legitimacy. This research concurs, and would only add that this ought to also improve third party chances. A small constituency is more likely to lean either left or right ideologically when compared to a large constituency. The law of averages causes more moderation as sample size increases and the median voter in a large constituency is more likely a true moderate. We learned in Chapter 1 that moderate ground is fertile ground for the already dominant political parties. Moreover, smaller constituencies would be more manageable for third parties to navigate. It was found in Chapters 2 and 3 that the primary reason that the Australian ballot caused a drop off in third party representation in Congress is that it did away with the opportunity for third parties to out-hustle the major political parties. Smaller constituencies would resurrect this possibility.

When constituencies are smaller, third parties have had some success in the United States. In recent years, the Green Party has been able to elect mayors to small and medium-size cities such as Marian City, Willits, and Sebastopol, California, along with Ward, Colorado, Langdon, Kansas, and the Village of Greenwich, and the Village of Victory in New York State. These constituencies are sufficiently small that an aggressive and competent third party candidate had a chance of winning. State legislative districts that were similarly sized might also prompt third party success. Once this level of experience became a reality, the successful third party candidate would have the "quality" that political scientists look for when judging electoral competence, and a much better chance of winning a seat in the United States House of Representatives.

Many people do not realize that the Founders of the United States Constitution intended for the size of the lower chamber to keep pace with the country's population growth. In fact, a constitutional amendment specifying this type of arrangement was proposed by Congress at the same time as the first ten Amendments to the Constitution. The states failed to ratify this amendment, representing a thorny constitutional question at the time because small states were worried about maintaining some semblance of equal representation in Congress. As it turns out, the lower chamber did grow from 65 members to 435 members over the first 124 years of United State's history. Then, a law passed in 1911, and subsequently upheld in 1929, froze the number of House seats at 435. Needless to say, the population did not stop growing in the early years of the 20th century.

Other Anglo-Saxon countries, with similar cultures and election rules as the United States have much larger legislatures. Table 6.1 exhibits the size of the Australian, Canadian, New Zealand, United Kingdom, and United States legislatures. Strikingly, the Canadian House of Lords (upper chamber) is larger than the United States Senate, while Canada has only about 11 percent of the total population of the United States. The size of the House of Lords in the United Kingdom is an anomaly, but the House of Commons in the

Table 6.1 The Size of Legislatures Relative to the Size of a Country's Population

Country	Chamber	Size of Legislature	Size of Population*	Ratio
Australia	House of Representatives	150	20,848,760	1 Rep. for every 138,991 people
	Senate	76	20,848,760	1 Rep. for every 274,325 people
Canada	House of Commons	308	33,873,357	1 Rep. for every 109,978 people
	House of Lords	105	33,873,357	1 Rep. for every 322,603 people
New Zealand	House of Representatives (unicameral)	122	4,143,279	1 Rep. for every 33,961 people
United Kingdom	House of Commons	650	60, 587,300	1 Rep. for every 93,211 people
	House of Lords	722	60, 587,300	1 Rep. for every 83,915 people
United States	House of Representatives	435	299,100,000	1 Rep. for every 687,586 people
	Senate	100	299,100,000	1 Rep. for every 2,991,000 people

* 2006 Population Estimates

United Kingdom is nearly 50 percent larger than the House of Representatives in the United States, but the United State's close ally across the Northern Atlantic has only 20 percent the population. In the United Kingdom there is approximately one representative in the House of Commons for every 93,000 people, while in the United States there is approximately one representative for every 687,000 people. Of the 650 members in the House of Commons in 2010, 89 of them (14 percent) represented nine different minor parties.

If the United States were to keep pace with the United Kingdom in reproducing a representative government, it would need to increase the size of the House of Representatives from 435 to 3208 members (see Table 6.2). Checking Table 6.2, in order for the United States to have the same level of representative government as exists in New Zealand, the House of Representatives would need to grow to 8807. The irony of the New Zealand value is that in New Zealand there is about one representative for every 33,000 people (see Table 6.1). When the United States Congress was first formed, the Founders had intended for there to be one member of the House of Representatives for every 30,000 people, approximately the same level of representation that exists in New Zealand today. The country of New Zealand uses a mixed election system with some seats selected by single-member district plurality rule elections and others

Table 6.2 The Size of the United States Congress if Constituencies were the Same Size as they are in Other Countries

Country	Projected Size	United States
Australia	2152	House of Representatives
	1090	Senate
Canada	2720	House of Representatives
	927	Senate
New Zealand	8807	House of Representatives
United Kingdom	3208	House of Representatives
	3564	Senate

by a form of proportional representation. In 2010, New Zealand has two major political parties—the National Party and the Labour Party—that hold 83 percent of all seats in their unicameral legislature. The remaining 17 percent of the seats are held by five different third parties. This level of third party representation in the United States in earlier eras, we learned in Chapter 4, was associated with considerable landmark legislative accomplishment.

It is also possible to expose the fallacy that the current size of legislatures in the United States is appropriate by examining state legislatures in the United States. Table 6.3 provides the same breakdown as Table 6.1, but simply includes the first five American states listed alphabetically. Examining Table 6.3, one can notice that Arkansas residents have nearly four times better representation than Arizona residents. If there were to be equity in citizen representation in state legislatures, the Arizona House of Representatives wound need to grow from 60 to 228 members and the Arizona state Senate from 30 to 80 seats. These smaller constituencies in Arizona might not be sufficient to produce successful third parties in the state. Reducing the size of constituencies may need to be coupled with other reforms to make this happen. After all, third parties have not fared well in Arkansas. The story about the size of state legislatures is told for a different reason. The discussion is intended to illustrate that there is little rhyme or reason to the size of legislatures in the United States.

Considering the lower chamber in Alaska, residents have over 26 times better representation than citizens of California. If the California lower chamber provided the same level of representation as the Alaskan lower chamber, it would need to seat 2117 members instead of 80. Is it any surprise that third parties have been much more viable in Alaska than they have been in California? Moreover, it is not surprising to learn that the two states that have the poorest level of representation in Table 6.3, Arizona and California, are two states that have had the fastest growing populations. People in the United States do not seem to concern themselves with the diluted representation that occurs as populations increase.

Table 6.3 The Size of State Legislatures Relative to the Size of a State's Population

State	Chamber	Size of Legislature	Size of Population*	Ratio
Alabama	House of Representatives	105	4,708,708	I Rep. for every 44,845 people
	Senate	35	4,708,708	I Rep. for every 134,535 people
Alaska	House of Representatives	40	698,473	I Rep. for every 17,462 people
	Senate	20	698,473	I Rep. for every 34,924 people
Arizona	House of Representatives	60	6,595,778	I Rep. for every 109,930 people
	Senate	30	6,595,778	I Rep. for every 219,860 people
Arkansas	House of Representatives	100	2,889,450	I Rep. for every 28,895 people
	Senate	35	2,889,450	I Rep. for every 82,556 people
California	House of Representatives	80	36,961,664	I Rep. for every 462,021 people
	Senate	40	36,961,664	I Rep. for every 924,042 people

* 2009 Population Estimates

As suggested above, it is not clear how small constituencies would need to be in order to prompt some reasonable level of third party success. What is clear is that the constituencies in the United Kingdom are sufficiently small that nationalist political parties from Wales, Scotland, and Northern Ireland are able to gain seats. What effect these third parties have on national debates in the United Kingdom is questionable. That citizens of these smaller constituencies appreciate having this "third" electoral option is not. No one voting for the candidates of these third parties in the United Kingdom thinks their party is going to hold a majority of the seats in the next parliament. What they do know is that their vote will not be wasted, because their district is sufficiently small to be able to elect one of their own. They may never be in the majority but they will enjoy representation nonetheless.

Conclusion

It is time to eliminate obviously restrictive local and state elections laws that make ballot access more difficult for third parties and independent candidates. Indeed, equal ballot access may be a necessary condition for third party electoral success. Yet, ballot access is not a sufficient condition to produce sustained third party electoral accomplishment. Third party advocates for too long have been hung up trying to gain ballot access without regard for broader arguments about what is truly causing their failure. In many instances, third party advocates seem oblivious to the reality that the deck of electoral cards is stacked against them, even when ballot access equity is not an issue. Green Party candidates in the state of Illinois in 2010 interviewed for this book amazingly seemed to hold the position that if only people better understood their message, qualifications, and promise, they would be successful. This admirable sentiment does not comport with the political/electoral realities that exist under single-member districts and plurality rule elections in the United States.

To date, the Green Party is decidedly left leaning, and with the two major political parties hugging the ideological center of large districts their electoral promise in SMD-PR elections is merely imaginary. The Green Party does not represent the median voter in the State of Illinois, or in any of the United States, and people would much rather not waste their vote on candidates that will lose. The same can be said for Libertarian Party candidates running throughout the country that lean too far to the right to be able to attract the median voter in large districts. The electoral promise of these two well-intentioned third parties is limited to local elections that use multi-member (at-large) districts or in small constituencies that lean their way ideologically. In small constituencies they may have a realistic chance to out-recruit the major party competition.

It is time for third party advocates to stop being fooled by false pretenses. The research presented in this book is not the first effort to try to awaken the consciousness of these well-minded reformers. Yet the message contained within this book still does not resonate and is still not fully appreciated by third party promoters. Still more, the truth and consequences of two-party dominance has not reached the attentive public, let alone the inattentive public.

What this chapter has been suggesting is not extreme or uncompromising. Nor are the changes proposed unrealistic. Much can be accomplished by an increase in public awareness. The fallacious and antiquated arguments used to prop up current election laws need to be exposed. How many people in the United States question the nature or character of election law? Going further, how many would defend them vehemently, out of a sense of patriotism, without having a clue what they are talking about? This is the problem. Too few people are aware of their options. Yet many are unsatisfied. Perhaps unknowingly they fail to recognize the truth and consequences of two-party dominance.

Notes

1 The Case for Third Party Representation

1. Data from the *Book of States* (Lexington, KY: Council of State Governments, 2008), 85–6. There are only 99 chambers in the 50 state legislatures because the state of Nebraska has a unicameral state legislature.
2. CBS News poll results were obtained from the Roper Center's "Topics at a Glance," provided by the Roper Center for Public Opinion Research, University of Connecticut.
3. Ibid.
4. Gary C. Jacobson, *The Politics of Congressional Elections*, 6th edition (New York: Longman, 2004), 41.
5. It is argued that same day registration laws in the state of Minnesota greatly benefitted Jesse Ventura's candidacy. People who had little history of voting were able to register to vote and cast a vote on Election Day. See Lisa Jane Disch, *The Tyranny of the Two-Party System* (New York: Columbia University Press, 2002), 1.
6. Ralph Nader made these comments in a speech on February 11, 2000 when he was announcing his bid for the Green Party presidential nomination. A full transcript of the speech had been available online at www.votenader.com/press/000221PresAnnounce.html, but is no longer accessible.
7. These comments were made by Pat Buchanan in an interview with John McLaughlin during his run for president as the Reform Party candidate in 2000. A full transcript of the interview had been available online at www.buchananreform.org/new/transcript/mclauglin_one_on_one, but is no longer accessible.
8. Anthony Downs, *An Economic Theory of Democracy* (New York: Harper Collins Publishers, 1957).
9. Benjamin Ginsberg, Theodore J. Lowi, and Margaret Weir, *We the People: An Introduction to American Politics*, 2nd edition (New York: W.W. Norton & Company, 1999), 243.
10. John Kingdom, "Models of Legislative Voting," *The Journal of Politics* 39 (1977): 563–95.
11. Ole R. Holsti, and James N. Rosenau, "Liberals, Populists, Libertarians, and Conservatives: The Link between Domestic and International Affairs," *International Political Science Review* 17 (1996): 29–54.
12. Benjamin Ginsberg, Theodore J. Lowi, and Margaret Weir, *We the People: An Introduction to American Politics*, 244.
13. Helmut Norpoth, "Explaining Party Cohesion in Congress: The Case of Shared Policy Attitudes," *American Political Science Review* 70 (1976): 1156–71.

14. John L. Sullivan, and Eric M. Uslander, "Congressional Behavior and Electoral Marginality," *American Journal of Political Science* 22 (1978): 536–53.
15. Scot Schraufnagel, and Jeffery J. Mondak, "The Issue Positions of House Democrats and Republicans: A Research Note," *Political Science Quarterly* 117 (2002): 479–90; John Aldrich, "Political Parties in a Critical Era," *American Politics Quarterly* 27 (1999): 9–32; Ian Budge, and Richard I. Hofferbert, "Mandates and Policy Outputs: U.S. Party Platforms and Federal Expenditures," *American Political Science Review* 84 (1990): 111–31.
16. Party line voting by Congress is made available by the *Congressional Quarterly Almanac*, which is now available on line at http://www.cqpress.com/lib/cq-almanac-online.html (last accessed August 10, 2010).
17. E.E. Schattschneider, *The Semisovereign People: A Realist's View of Democracy in America* (New York: Holt, Rinehart, and Winston, Inc, 1960), 86.
18. Ibid., 88–93.
19. Scot Schraufnagel, and Jeffery J. Mondak, "The Issue Positions of House Democrats and Republicans: A Research Note."
20. Ibid., 489.
21. Ibid., 489.
22. Source: Data compiled by author.
23. Pew research Center/National Journal Congressional Connection Poll, July 2010. Retrieved August 5, 2010 from the iPoll Databank, the Roper Center for Public Opinion Research, University of Connecticut. http://www.ropercenter.uconn.edu/dta_access/ipoll/ipoll.html.
24. Ibid.
25. Ibid
26. John F. Bibby, and L. Sandy Maisel, *Two-Parties-or More?: The American Party System*, 2nd edition (Boulder, CO: Westview Press, 2003), 57–8.
27. Austin, Ranney, *The Doctrine of Responsible Party Government: Its Origins and Present State* (Urbana, IL: The University of Illinois Press, 1954).
28. E.E. Schattschneider, *The Semisovereign People.*
29. Shaun Bowler, and Daivd J. Lanoue, "New Party Challenges and Partisan Change: The Effects of Party Competition on Party Loyalty," *Political Behavior* 18 (1996): 327–43; Josephine T. Andrews, and Robert W. Jackman, "If Winning Isn't Everything, Why Do They Keep Score? Consequences of Electoral Performance for Party Leaders," *British Journal of Political Science* 38 (2008): 657–75. A two-and-one-half party system also exists in the Federal Republic of Germany, which uses some proportional representation elections.
30. The arguments are those put forward in John F. Bibby, and L. Sandy Maisel, *Two-Parties-or More?: The American Party System*, 111–20.
31. For arguments about the need to increase the size of the national legislature in the United States see Brian Fredrick, *Congressional Representation & Constituents: The Case for Increasing the U.S. House of Representatives* (New York: Routledge, 2010).
32. Gary C. Jacobson, *The Politics of Congressional Elections*, 16; Marjorie Randon Hershey, *Party Politics in America*, 12th edition (New York: Longman Classics, 2007), Chapters 9 and 10.
33. Ibid.
34. Ibid.
35. Lawrence C. Dodd, and Scot Schraufnagel, "Congress, Civility and Legislative Productivity: A Historical Perspective," in *Congress Reconsidered*, 9th edition, eds. Lawrence C. Dodd and Bruce I. Oppenheimer (Washington, DC: Congressional Quarterly Press, 2009).

2 The Effect of Election Laws on Third Party Failure

1. Eldon C. Evans, *A History of the Australian Ballot System in the United States* (Chicago, IL: University of Chicago Press, 1917); Shigeo Hirano, and James M. Snyder, Jr., "The Decline of Third-Party Voting in the United States," *Journal of Politics* 69 (2007): 1–16.

2. Maurice Duverger, *Political Parties, Their Organization and Activity in the Modern State* (New York: Wiley, 1954); William H. Riker, "The Number of Political Parties: A Reexamination of Duverger's Law," *Comparative Politics* 9 (1976): 93–106.

3. Marjorie Randon Hershey, *Party Politics in America*, 12th edition (New York: Longman Classics, 2007), 121.

4. ibid., 196.

5. Hirano and Snyder, "The Decline of Third-Party Voting in the United States"; Barry C. Burden, "Ballot Regulations and Multiparty Politics in the States," *PS* 40 (2007): 669–73; Theodore J. Lowi, "Toward a More Responsible Three-Party System: The Mythology of the Two Party System and the Prospects for Reform," *PS* 16 (1983): 699–706.

6. Paul Herrnson, "Two-Party Dominance and Minor Party Forays in American Politics," in *Multiparty Politics in America*, eds. Paul S. Herrnson and John C. Green (Lanham, MD: Rowman and Littlefield Publishers, 1997); Richard Winger, "Institutional Obstacles to a Multiparty System," in *Multiparty Politics in America*, eds. Paul S. Herrnson and John C. Green, (Lanham, MD: Rowman and Littlefield Publishers, 1997); Theodore J. Lowi, "Toward a Responsible Three-Party System: Plan or Obituary?" in *The State of the Parties*, eds. John C. Green and Daniel M. Shea (Lanham, MD: Rowman and Littlefield Publishers, 1999); Paul S. Herrnson, "Minor-Party Candidates in Congressional Elections," in *The Marketplace of Democracy: Electoral Competition and American Politics*, eds. Michael P. McDonald and John Samples (Washington DC: Brookings Institution Press, 2006).

7. Much of the third party voting literature documents the types of individuals that are more or less likely to vote for minor party candidates in presidential elections, see Sheldon Kamieniecku, "The Dimensionality of Partisan Strength and Political Independence," *Political Behavior* 10 (1988): 364–76; Howard J. Gold, "Third Party Voting in Presidential Elections: A Study of Perot, Anderson, and Wallace," *Political Research Quarterly* 48 (1995): 751–73; Steven J. Rosenstone, Roy L. Behr, and Edward H. Lazarus, *Third Parties in America*, 2nd edition (Princeton, NJ: Princeton University Press, 1996), Chapters 6 and 8; Paul R. Abramson, John H. Aldrich, Phillip Paolino, and David W. Rohde, "Challenges to the American Two-Party System: Evidence from the 1968, 1980, 1992, and 1996 Presidential Elections," *Political Research Quarterly* 53 (2000): 495–522. Others look at individual-level voting in gubernatorial elections, see Dean Lacy, and Quin Monson, "The Origins and Impact of Votes for Third-Party Candidates: A Case Study of the 1998 Minnesota Gubernatorial Election," *Political Research Quarterly* 55 (2002): 409–37. It is found that third party voters tend to be weak partisans or political independents, see Howard J Gold, "Third Party Voting in Presidential Elections: A Study of Perot, Anderson, and Wallace," with low levels of trust in government, see Shaun Bowler, and David J. Lanoue, "Strategic and Protest Voting for Third Parties: The Case of the Canadian NDP," *The Western Political Quarterly* 45 (1992): 485–99; Geoff Peterson, and J. Mark Wrighton, "Expressions of Distrust: Third-Party Voting and Cynicism in Government," *Political Behavior* 20 (1998): 17–34; Dean Lacy and Quin Monson, "The Origins and Impact of Votes for Third-Party Candidates: A Case Study of the 1998 Minnesota Gubernatorial Election,"

who believe that the nation is on the wrong track, see Barbara Norrander, "Explaining Cross-State Variation in Independent Identification," *American Journal of Political Science* 33 (1989): 516–36; Howard J. Gold, "Third Party Voting in Presidential Elections: A Study of Perot, Anderson, and Wallace"; Steven J. Rosenstone et al., *Third Parties in America*, Ch. 6; Paul R. Abramson et al., "Challenges to the American Two-Party System: Evidence from the 1968, 1980, 1992, and 1996 Presidential Elections." Others have argued that third party voting is not so much muted through electoral laws, but rather that third party issues are absorbed into major party platforms once they reach a certain level of public awareness, effectively cutting off third party lifelines, see Barry C. Burden, "Ballot Regulations and Multiparty Politics in the States"; Shigeo Hirano and James M. Snyder, "The Decline of Third-Party Voting in the United States."

8. See Bruce W. Robeck, and James A. Dyer, "Ballot Access Requirements in Congressional Elections," *American Politics Research* 10 (1982): 31–45; Barbara Norrander, "Explaining Cross-State Variation in Independent Identification"; Mark R. Brown, "Popularizing Ballot Access: The Front Door to Election Reform," *Ohio State Law Journal* 58 (1997): 1281–324; Thomas Stratmann, "Ballot Access Restrictions and Candidate Entry in Elections," *European Journal of Political Economy* 21 (2005): 59–71; Barry C. Burden, "Ballot Regulations and Multiparty Politics in the States."

9. Barbara Norrander, "Explaining Cross-State Variation in Independent Identification."

10. Daniel A. Mazmanian, *Third Parties in Presidential Elections* (Washington, DC: Brookings Institution, 1974); Frank Smallwood, *The Other Candidates: Third Parties in Presidential Elections* (Hanover, NH: University Press of New England, 1983); Howard J. Gold, "Third Party Voting in Presidential Elections: A Study of Perot, Anderson, and Wallace"; Michael S. Lewis-Beck, and Peverill Squire, "The Politics of Institutional Choice: Presidential Ballot Access for Third Parties in the United States," *British Journal of Political Science* 25 (1995): 419–27; Dean Lacy and Quin Monson, "The Origins and Impact of Votes for Third-Party Candidates: A Case Study of the 1998 Minnesota Gubernatorial Election"; Neal Allen, and Brian J. Brox, "The Roots of Third Party Voting: The 2000 Nader Campaign in Historical Perspective," *Party Politics* 11 (2005): 623–37; Barry C. Burden, "Minor Parties and Strategic Voting in Recent U.S. Presidential Elections," *Electoral Studies* 24 (2005): 603–18; Barry C. Burden, "Ballot Regulations and Multiparty Politics in the States."

11. For exceptions see Bruce W. Robeck, and James A. Dyer, "Ballot Access Requirements in Congressional Elections"; Paul S. Herrnson, "Minor-Party Candidates in Congressional Elections"; Shigeo Hirano, and James M. Snyder, Jr., "The Decline of Third-Party Voting in the United States"; and Bernard Tamas, and Matthew Hindman, "Do State Election Laws Really Hurt Third Parties? Ballot Access, Fusion and Elections to the U.S. House of Representatives" (paper presented at the Midwest Political Science Association. Chicago, IL), 2007.

12. Glenn R. Parker, *Congress and the Rent-Seeking Society* (Ann Arbor, MI: University of Michigan Press, 1996).

13. David Rohde, *Parties and Leaders in the Postreform House* (Chicago, IL: University of Chicago Press, 1991).

14. This reinforces the finding that the electoral institutional playground is not driving third party or independent electoral success. Instead when third party or independent candidates have been successful in the modern era there are peculiar (non-systematic) explanations for their success.

15. Michael S. Lewis-Beck, and Peverill Squire, "The Politics of Institutional Choice: Presidential Ballot Access for Third Parties in the United States"; Stephen

Ansolabehere, and Alan Gerber, "The Effects of Filing Fees and Petition Requirements on U.S. House Elections," *Legislative Studies Quarterly* 21 (1996): 249–64; Diana Dwyre, and Robin Kolodny, "Barriers to Minor Party Success and Prospects for Change, in *Multiparty Politics in American*, eds. Paul S. Herrnson and John C. Green (Lanham, MD: Rowman and Littlefield Publishers, 1997).

16. Joshua E. Rosenkranz, "Voter Choice '96: A 50 State Report Card on the Presidential Elections" (Brennan Center for Justice at New York University School of Law, 1996).

17. The hypothetical range of this variable is 0 to 162. Changes in ballot access laws were obtained from *Ballot Access News* at http://www.ballot-access.org/ (last access August 12, 2010).

18. Steve Cobble, and Sarah Siskind, *Fusion: Multiple Party Nomination in the United States* (Washington, DC: Center for a New Democracy, 2003); Peter H. Argersinger, "A Place on the Ballot: Fusion Politics and Antifusion Laws," *American Historical Review* 85 (1980): 289–306.

19. William H. Riker, "The Number of Political Parties: A Reexamination of Duverger's Law"; Howard A. Scarrow, "Duverger's Law, Fusion, and the Decline of American 'Third' Parties," *Western Political Quarterly* 39 (1986): 634–47.

20. Howard A. Scarrow, "Duverger's Law, Fusion, and the Decline of American 'Third' Parties," 644.

21. In alternative model runs, not presented in this chapter, both fusion ban variables were included in the same models. This specification rendered the "Fusion Directly Banned" statistically insignificant, while the practice of "Fusion Indirectly Banned" remained significant. The research also created a fourth measure of the effects of fusion. In this instance, the variable was coded "1" if fusion is allowed, "–1" if fusion is directly banned, and "0" otherwise. This test returns a statistically significant association between fusion and non-major party voting in all model runs and does not change the statistical significance of other variables in the models. Fusion laws for the 50 states are available at Ballot Access News http://www.ballot-access.org/ (last accessed August 12, 2010).

22. Malcolme E. Jewell, *Parties and Primaries* (New York: Praeger Publishers, 1984).

23. Barbara Norrander, "Explaining Cross-State Variation in Independent Identification."

24. Classifications of state primary systems are available from the PEW Center on the States at: http://www.pewcenteronthestates.org (last accessed August 12, 2010).

25. Maurice Duverger, *Political Parties, Their Organization and Activity in the Modern State*, 216–17.

26. Ideally, additional data points for self-identified Independents would be available. However, the best source for this data is the National Election Study. Unfortunately, there is no survey respondents from many states during the time period studied. Other sources are either incomplete or not as routinely cited as the values calculated by Gerald C. Wright, Robert S. Erikson, and John P. McIver, "Measuring State Partisanship and Ideology with Survey Data," *The Journal of Politics* 47 (1985): 469–89. To avoid potential problems associated with mixing data sources only the single data point is used.

27. See Sheldon Kamieniecku, "The Dimensionality of Partisan Strength and Political Independence"; Barbara Norrander, "Explaining Cross-State Variation in Independent Identification."

28. It has been found in previous work that states with a stronger single or one-party tradition offer less electoral support for third parties. Michael J. Dubin, *Party Affiliations in the State Legislatures: A Year by Year Summary, 1796–2006* (Jefferson, NC: McFarland and Company, 2007). The values for 2008 were calculated by the author.

29. Shaun Bowler, and David J. Lanoue, "Strategic and Protest Voting for Third Parties: The Case of the Canadian NDP"; Geoff Peterson, and J. Mark Wrighton, "Expressions of Distrust: Third-Party Voting and Cynicism in Government."

30. The ideology scores created range from "0" (more conservative) to "1" (more liberal) and are developed using identical scaling. See William D. Berry, Even J. Ringquist, Richard C. Fording, and Russell L. Hanson, "Measuring Citizen and Government Ideology in the American States, 1960–93," *American Journal of Political Science* 42 (1998): 327–48.

31. Lisa Jane Disch, *The Tyranny of the Two-Party System* (New York: Columbia University Press, 2002).

32. The ten states that currently allow fusion candidacies are AR, CT, DE, ID, MS, NY, SC. SD, UT, and VT.

33. Barbara Norrander, "Explaining Cross-State Variation in Independent Identification," 534–35.

34. See Barry C. Burden, and Steven Greene, "Party Attachments and State Election Laws."

35. Anecdotally, personal resources allowed minor party candidates such as Governor Jesse Ventura and presidential candidate Ross Perot to overcome obstacles in their independent candidacies. Moreover, the previous political experience of Bernard Sanders (I-VT), a former minor party mayor, and Senator Joe Lieberman (I-CT) likely facilitated their electoral success as non-major party candidates.

36. Joseph Cooper, "From Congressional to Presidential Preeminence: Power and Politics in Late Nineteenth-Century America and Today," in *Congress Reconsidered*, 9th edition, eds. Lawrence C. Dodd and Bruce I. Oppenheimer (Washington, DC: Congressional Quarterly Press, 2009), 362.

37. J. Scott Long, *Regression Models for Categorical and Limited Dependent Variable* (Thousand Oaks, CA: Sage Publications, 1997), 187.

38. John F. McDonald, and Robert A. Moffitt, "The Uses of Tobit Analysis," *Review of Economics and Statistics* 62 (1980): 318–21; J. Scott Long, *Regression Models for Categorical and Limited Dependent Variable*, 189.

39. Nathaniel Beck, and Jonathan N. Katz, "What to do (and not to do) with Time-Series Cross-Section Data," *American Political Science Review* 89 (1995): 634–47.

40. Stata Corporation, "Xttobit: Random Effects Tobit Models," available at http://www.stata.com/help.cgi?quadchk (last accessed August 12, 2010).

3 More of the Truth: Ballot Access Reform in Maryland and Florida

1. Steve Cobble, and Sarah Siskind, *Fusion: Multiple Party Nomination in the United States* (Washington, DC: Center for a New Democracy, 2003); Howard A. Scarrow, "Duverger's Law, Fusion, and the Decline of American 'Third' Parties," *Western Political Quarterly* 39 (1986): 634–47, see page 644.

2. See Bruce W. Robeck, and James A. Dyer, "Ballot Access Requirements in Congressional Elections," *American Politics Research* 10 (1982): 31–45; Stephen Ansolabehere, and Alan Gerber, "The Effects of Filing Fees and Petition Requirements on U.S. House Elections," *Legislative Studies Quarterly* 21 (1996): 249–64; Diana Dwyre, and Robin Kolodny, "Barriers to Minor Party Success and Prospects for Change," in *Multiparty Politics in American*, eds. Paul S. Herrnson and John C. Green (Lanham, MD: Rowman and Littlefield Publishers, 1997); Richard Winger, "Institutional Obstacles to a Multiparty System," in *Multiparty

Politics in America, eds. Paul S. Herrnson, and John C. Green (Lanham, MD: Rowman and Littlefield Publishers, 1997); Theodore J. Lowi, "Toward a Responsible Three-Party System: Plan or Obituary?" in *The State of the Parties*, eds. John C. Green, and Daniel M. Shea, (Lanham, MD: Rowman and Littlefield Publishers, 1999); Steve Cobble, and Sarah Siskind, *Fusion: Multiple Party Nomination in the United States*; Thomas Stratmann, "Ballot Access Restrictions and Candidate Entry in Elections," *European Journal of Political Economy* 21 (2005): 59–71.

3. Michael S. Lewis-Beck, and Peverill Squire, "The Politics of Institutional Choice: Presidential Ballot Access for Third Parties in the United States," *British Journal of Political Science* 25 (1995): 419–27; Joshua E. Rosenkranz, "Voter Choice '96: A 50 State Report Card on the Presidential Elections (Brennan Center for Justice at New York University School of Law, 1996); Diana Dwyre and Robin Kolodny, "Barriers to Minor Party Success and Prospects for Change"; Richard Winger, "Institutional Obstacles to a Multiparty System."

4. Eric Boehlert, "Al's Ballot Blues," *Open Salon*, 2000, http://www.salon.com/news/politics/feature/2000/11/16/ballots/print.html (last accessed August 15, 2010).

5. Richard Winger, "Florida Voters Wipe Out Mandatory Petitions," *Ballot Access News*, Volume 14 Number 8 (1998); Richard Sommerville, and Christina Clemenson, "Improving Ballot Access in Florida," *Green Party of Florida*, 1998, http://www.greens.org/s-r/17/17–05.html (last accessed August 15, 2010).

6. Richard Winger, "Florida Voters Wipe Out Mandatory Petitions."

7. Eric Boehlert, "Al's Ballot Blues."

8. Deborah O'Neil, "Third Parties Push for Equal Access to Ballot," *St. Petersburg Times*, August 3, 1998.

9. Eric Boehlert, "Al's Ballot Blues."

10. Myriam, Marquez, "Want to Live in a True Democracy? Vote for Open Elections," *Orlando Sentinel*, September 14, 1998, A12.

11. Richard Sommerville, and Christina Clemenson, "Improving Ballot Access in Florida;" Richard Winger, "Florida Voters Wipe Out Mandatory Petitions."

12. Deborah O'Neil, "Third Parties Push for Equal Access to Ballot."

13. Richard Winger, "Florida Voters Wipe Out Mandatory Petitions."

14. The measure also provided that candidates for the governor's office may run in primary elections without identifying a selection for lieutenant governor; corrected the voting age in Florida to 18 to coincide with the U.S. Constitution; provided for public financing of political campaigns if the candidates who avail themselves of the benefit agree to set spending limits; made school board elections non-partisan; and allowed all voters to cast votes in primary elections regardless of party affiliation if the winner of that contest will run unopposed in the general election, Florida Department of State (1998).

15. Deborah O'Neil, "Third Parties Push for Equal Access to Ballot."

16. Robert Perez, "Polling Sites Could Get Crowded," *Orlando Sentinel*, November 12, 1998.

17. The Florida Senate moved to Republican Party Control in 1992 and the Florida House of Representatives in 1996, and the Republican Party has been comfortably in control of both chambers since this time.

18. David Goldsmith, *A History of the Maryland Greens: 1990–2003* (San Francisco, CA: Ruby Skye, 2004).

19. Richard Winger, "Ballot Access: Good Bills Die," *Ballot Access News*, Volume 12 Number 2 (1996).

20. Richard Winger, "Maryland Bill Signed," *Ballot Access News*, Volume 14 Number 3 (1998).

21. All non-major party voting is included in the dependent variable because non-major party voting is the phenomenon of primary theoretical interest. Spoiled ballots, however, are not included in either the numerator or the denominator when calculating the percentage of votes cast. These are ballots that were cast, but not counted, due to a number of reasons including voting for more than one candidate for the same office or marking the ballot in such a manner that voter intent cannot be clearly determined.

22. Marjorie Randon Hershey, *Party Politics in America*, 12th edition (New York: Longman, 2007), 114.

23. See Michael R. Alvarez, and Jonathan Nagler, "Economics, Issues and the Perot Candidacy: Voter Choice in the 1992 Presidential Election," *American Journal of Political Science* 39 (1995): 714–44; Howard J. Gold, "Third Party Voting in Presidential Elections: A Study of Perot, Anderson, and Wallace," *Political Research Quarterly* 48 (1995): 751–73.

24. It must be noted that Tobit coefficients represent the effect of x on latent y (or y^*) and not the observed y, see Dennis W. Roneck, "Learning More from Tobit Coefficients: Extending a Comparative Analysis of Political Protest," *American Sociological Review* 57 (1992): 503–07. In this case, of interest is the expected value of y conditional on y being greater than zero. In order to obtain this value one must calculate the marginal effects of x on y, if y is greater than zero. This can be done using the "dtobit" command in Stata 9. It is the conditional effects of x on y that are reported in Table 3.1.

25. A similar result was obtained when researchers tried to tie political independence to support for third party candidates in all the American states, see Barbara Norrander, "Explaining Cross-State Variation in Independent Identification," *American Journal of Political Science* 33 (1989): 516–36; Barry C. Burden, and Steven Greene, "Party Attachments and State Election Laws," *Political Research Quarterly* 53 (2000): 63–76.

26. Marjorie Randon Hershey, *Party Politics in America*, 114.

27. Greg D. Adams, "Legislative Effects of Single-Member vs. Multi-Member Districts," *American Journal of Political Science* 40 (1996): 129–44.

28. For the 1964 election the entire state of Illinois was a single House district, see Michael J. Dubin, *Party Affiliations in the State Legislatures: A Year by Year Summary, 1796–2006* (Jefferson, NC: McFarland and Company, 2007). This was a temporary response to the Supreme Court ruling that established the "one person one vote" principle, see Greg D. Adams, "Legislative Effects of Single-Member vs. Multi-Member Districts." It can also be noted that minor parties have held about 1.5 percent of the state legislative seats in Massachusetts between 1857 and 2006; a state that allows for some multi-member districts, see Michael J. Dubin, *Party Affiliations in the State Legislatures: A Year by Year Summary.*

4 Third Parties and Landmark Policy Productivity

1. For a more complete discussion of the hypothesized relationship between moderate conflict and landmark legislative productivity see Lawrence C. Dodd, and Scot Schraufnagel, "Congress, Civility and Legislative Productivity: A Historical Perspective," in *Congress Reconsidered*, 9th edition, eds. Lawrence C. Dodd and Bruce I. Oppenheimer (Washington, DC: Congressional Quarterly Press, 2009).

2. Steven S. Smith, and Gerald Gamm, "The Dynamics of Party Government in Congress," in *Congress Reconsidered*, 9th edition, eds. Lawrence C. Dodd and Bruce I. Oppenheimer (Washington, DC: Congressional Quarterly Press, 2009).

3. Joseph Cooper, and David W. Brady, "Institutional Context and Leadership Style: The House from Cannon to Rayburn," *American Political Science Review* 75 (1981): 411–25; David W. Rohde, *Parties and Leaders in the Postreform House* (Chicago, IL: University of Chicago Press, 1991); Gary W. Cox, and Mathew D. McCubbins, *Setting the Agenda. Responsible Party Government in the US House of Representatives* (Cambridge, MA and New York: Cambridge University Press, 2005); Keith Poole, and Howard Rosenthal, *Congress: A Political-Economic History of Roll Call Voting* (New York: Oxford University Press, 1997); Steven S. Smith, and Gerald Gamm, "The Dynamics of Party Government in Congress."

4. Barbara Sinclair, *Unorthodox Lawmaking: New Legislative Processes in the U.S. Congress* (Washington, DC: CQ Press, 1997), Chapter 6.

5. Significant Clean Air Act amendments were passed in December 1970 and the Federal Water Pollution Control Acts of 1972 greatly enhanced government enforcement of minimal water quality standards.

6. David R. Mayhew, *Divided We Govern: Party Control, Lawmaking, and Investigations, 1946–1990* (New Haven, CT: Yale University Press, 1991).

7. Moderate when compared to the late 1940s and 1950s and the contemporary period.

8. David R. Mayhew, *Divided We Govern: Party Control, Lawmaking, and Investigations, 1946–1990*; Sarah Binder, *Stalemate: Causes and Consequences of Legislative Gridlock, 1947–96* (Washington, DC: Brookings, 2003); Joshua Clinton, and John Lapinski, "Measuring Legislative Accomplishment, 1877–1994," *American Journal of Political Science* 50 (2006): 232–49.

9. For a discussion of the relationship between party homogeneity and the relative strength of political party leaders see the work on "conditional party government" by David W. Rohde, *Parties and Leaders in the Postreform House*; John H. Aldrich, and David W. Rohde, "The Logic of Conditional Party Government: Revisiting the Electoral Connection," in *Congress Reconsidered*, 7th edition, eds. Lawrence C. Dodd, and Bruce I. Oppenheimer. (Washington, DC: CQ Press, 2001).

10. Lawrence C. Dodd, and Scot Schraufnagel, "Congress, Civility and Legislative Productivity: A Historical Perspective."

11. There has been a great deal of scholarly attention paid to the issue of legislative gridlock. For a sampling of this literature see, Patricia A. Hurley, "Assessing the Potential for Significant Legislative Output in the House of Representatives," *Western Political Quarterly* 32 (1979): 45–58; David R. Mayhew, *Divided We Govern: Party Control, Lawmaking, and Investigations, 1946–1990*; Sean Q. Kelly, "Divided We Govern: A Reassessment," *Polity* 25 (1993): 475–84; George C. Edwards III, Andrew Barrett, and Jeffrey Peake, "The Legislative Impact of Divided Government," *American Journal of Political Science* 41 (1997): 545–63; David W. Brady, and Craig Volden, *Revolving Gridlock: Politics and Policy from Carter to Clinton* (Boulder, CO: Westview Press, 1997); John J. Coleman, "Unified Government, Divided Government, and Party Responsiveness," *American Political Science Review* 93 (1999): 821–35; William Howell, Scott Adler, Charles Cameron, and Charles Riemann, "Divided Government and the Legislative Productivity of Congress, 1945–94," *Legislative Studies Quarterly* 25 (2000): 285–312; David R. Jones, "Party Polarization and Legislative Gridlock," *Political Research Quarterly* 54 (2001): 125–41; Sarah Binder, *Stalemate: Causes and Consequences of Legislative Gridlock, 1947–96*.

12. See Keith Krehbiel, "Institutional and Partisan Sources of Gridlock: A Theory of Divided and Unified Government," *Journal of Theoretical Politics* 8 (1996): 7–40.

13. David R. Mayhew, *Divided We Govern: Party Control, Lawmaking, and Investigations, 1946–1990*; Morris P. Fiorina, "Split Party Government in the American States: A Byproduct of Legislative Professionalism," *American Political Science Review* 88 (1994): 304–16.

14. John J. Coleman, "Unified Government, Divided Government, and Party Responsiveness"; Sarah Binder, *Stalemate: Causes and Consequences of Legislative Gridlock.*

15. Lawrence C. Dodd, and Scot Schraufnagel, "Congress, Civility and Legislative Productivity: A Historical Perspective."

16. For instance, it was argued in Chapter 1 that the electoral support obtained by third party presidential candidate Ross Perot prompted legislative innovation even though he was not ultimately successful in his bid to capture the White House.

17. For the purposes of this examination, members of Congress who are identified as independents and are not affiliated with any organized political party were excluded from consideration. The focus of much of this research is on actual third parties as opposed to those who operate independent of political parties.

18. In the case studies that follow, the Roosevelt-Progressives (1913–19) and the La Follette Progressives (1935–40) will be considered two different cases.

19. For an alternative approach to measuring legislative accomplishment across long historical time frames, see the work of Joshua Clinton, and John Lapinski, "Measuring Legislative Accomplishment, 1877–1994." Their work uses 20 elite evaluations of legislative enactments and an item-response model to integrate the information contained in the ratings and establish "legislative accomplishment" Congress by Congress.

20. The vast majority of the entries are public laws; however, joint resolutions that propose amendments to the Constitution are also included. Admission of new states and declarations of war are also included if they are mentioned in the sources consulted.

21. An additional 12 pieces of legislation are mentioned in either 13 or 14 of the 15 sources.

22. Valerie Heitschusen, and Garry Young, "Macropolitics and Changes in the U.S. Code: Testing Competing Theories of Policy Production, 1874–1946," in *The Macropolitics of Congress*, eds. E. Scott Adler and John S. Lapinski (Princeton, N.J.: Princeton University Press, 2006).

23. See David R. Mayhew, *Divided We Govern: Party Control, Lawmaking, and Investigations, 1946–1990*; Sarah Binder, *Stalemate: Causes and Consequences of Legislative Gridlock, 1947–96.* The strongest correlations occur between Landmark Laws and David Mayhew's measure. In this instance, the correlation climbs to $r = .76$. The Binder "Gridlock 1" measure correlates with Landmark Laws at $r = -.65$. The correlation is negative because her measure is of gridlock and not productivity. Both measures of productivity created for this research, during the post-World War II period, are more highly correlated with Mayhew and Binder than they are with each other.

24. This examination of each third party and each landmark law in the database on an individual basis has tangible benefits that could not be easily achieved using a quantitative study of the contribution to legislative productivity made by third parties. The qualitative analysis allows for careful consideration of each third party and each issue to better determine any specific relationship between the third party and the passage of the landmark laws.

25. Earle Dudley Ross, *The Liberal Republican Movement* (New York: Henry Holt and Company, 1919).

26. Richard Allen Gerber, "The Liberal Republicans of 1872 in Historiographical Perspective," *The Journal of American History* 61 (1975): 40–73.

27. Earle Dudley Ross, *The Liberal Republican Movement*; Richard Allen Gerber, "The Liberal Republicans of 1872 in Historiographical Perspective"; Matthew T. Downey, "Horace Greeley and the Politicians: The Liberal Republican Convention in 1872," *The Journal of American History* 53 (1967): 727–50.

28. Ibid.
29. Earle Dudley Ross, *The Liberal Republican Movement.*
30. The rights of ex-confederates to hold office were never officially repealed from the Fourteenth Amendment. Troop withdrawal from the South did not take place until the Compromise of 1877, which settled the contested 1876 presidential election on the understanding that newly elected President Rutherford B. Hayes would remove national government troops that were propping up Republican Party state governments in South Carolina, Florida, and Louisiana.
31. Herbert J. Clancy, *The Presidential Election of 1880* (Chicago, IL: Loyola University Press, 1958); Matthew Hild, *Greenbackers, Knights of Labor, and Populists: Farmer-Labor Insurgency in the Late-nineteenth-century South* (Athens, GA: University of Georgia Press, 2007).
32. Herbert J. Clancy, *The Presidential Election of 1880;* Irwin Unger, *The Greenback Era: A Social and Political History of American Finance, 1865–1879* (Princeton, NJ: Princeton University Press, 1964); Matthew Hild, *Greenbackers, Knights of Labor, and Populists; Farmer-Labor.*
33. Herbert J. Clancy, *The Presidential Election of 1880.*
34. Gwendolyn Mink, *New Immigration in American Political Development; Union, Party, and State, 1875–1920* (Ithaca, NY: Cornell University Press, 1986).
35. Vincent P. De Santis, *Republicans Face the Southern Question: The New Departure Years* (Baltimore, MD: Johns Hopkins Press, 1959); Charles Chilton Pearson, *The Readjuster Movement in Virginia* (New Haven, CT: Yale University Press, 1969); Jane Dailey, *Before Jim Crow: The Politics of Race in Postemancipation Virginia* (Chapel Hill, NC: University of North Carolina Press, 2000).
36. Charles Chilton Pearson, *The Readjuster Movement in Virginia.*
37. Ibid.; Jane Dailey, *Before Jim Crow: The Politics of Race in Postemancipation Virginia.*
38. Lawrence Goodwyn, *The Populist Movement: A Short History of the Agrarian Revolt in America* (Oxford, UK: Oxford Press, 1978); Michael Kazin, *The Populist Persuasion: An American History* (New York: Basic Books, 1995).
39. William Alfred Peffer, *Populism, Its Rise and Fall* (Lawrence, KS: University Press of Kansas, 1992).
40. Matthew Hild, *Greenbackers, Knights of Labor, and Populists: Farmer-Labor Insurgency in the Late-nineteenth-century South.*
41. Lawrence Goodwyn, *The Populist Movement: A Short History of the Agrarian Revolt in America;* William Alfred Peffer, *Populism, Its Rise and Fall;* Michael Kazin, *The Populist Persuasion: An American History.*
42. James L. Hunt, *Marion Butler and American Populism* (Chapel Hill, NC: University of North Carolina Press, 2003).
43. James A. Henretta, David Brody, Lynn Dumenil, and Susan Ware, *America's History,* 5th edition (Boston, MA: Bedford/St. Martin, 2004), 536–38.
44. Mary Ellen Glass, *Silver and Politics in Nevada: 1892–1902* (Reno, NV: University of Nevada Press, 1969).
45. Rebecca Edwards, *The Silver Party* (Poughkeepsie, NY: Vassar College, 2000), http://en.wikipedia.org/wiki/Silver_Party (last accessed September 3, 2010).
46. Ibid.
47. Mary Ellen Glass, *Silver and Politics in Nevada: 1892–1902.*
48. "Senate Passes Currency Bill," *New York Times,* February 16, 1900, 1.
49. John A. Gable, *The Bull Moose Years: Theodore Roosevelt and the Progressive Party* (Port Washington, NY: Kenniket Press, 1978); James Chace, *Wilson, Roosevelt, Taft, and Debs—the Election That Changed the Country* (New York: Simon and Schuster, 2004).
50. Robert S. La Forte, "Theodore Roosevelt's Osawatomie Speech," *Kansas Historical Quarterly* 32 (1966): 187–200.

51. George Edwin Mowry, *Theodore Roosevelt and the Progressive Movement* (New York: Hill and Wang, 1960); James Chace, *Wilson, Roosevelt, Taft, and Debs—the Election That Changed the Country.*

52. John A. Gable, *The Bull Moose Years: Theodore Roosevelt and the Progressive Party.*

53. Amos Pinchot, *History of the Progressive Party, 1912–1916* (New York: New York University Press, 1958).

54. The national party organization largely falls apart following the 1914 midterm elections, which saw only six party members win seats in the House of Representatives. While Roosevelt was nominated for president once again in 1916, he quickly withdrew from the race to support Republican candidate Charles Evan Hughes. This election saw the last of the Bull Moose members elected to the House.

55. "Wilson Kept Pledges," *New York Times*, August 30, 1916, 5.

56. E.E. Schattschneider, *The Semisovereign People: A Realist's View of Democracy in America* (New York: Holt, Rinehart, and Winston, Inc, 1960), 86.

57. Jonathon Kasparek, *Fighting Son: A Biography of Philip F. La Follette* (Madison, WI: Wisconsin Historical Society Press, 2006).

58. Paul W. Glad, *The History of Wisconsin, Volume V: War, A New Era, and Depression, 1914–1940* (Madison, WI: Wisconsin State Historical Society Press, 1990); Jonathon Kasparek, *Fighting Son: A Biography of Phillip F. La Follette.*

59. Lawrence C. Dodd, and Scot Schraufnagel, "Congress, Civility and Legislative Productivity: A Historical Perspective."

60. Keith Poole, Data Download (University of Georgia: Athens, GA), http://www.voteview.com/dwnl.htm (last accessed September 3, 2010).

61. James L. Sundquist, *The Decline and Resurgence of Congress* (Washington DC: The Brookings Institute, 1981), 25–30; Sarah A. Binder, "The Partisan Basis of Procedural Choice: Allocating Parliamentary Rights in the House, 1789–1991," *American Political Science Review* 90 (1996): 8–20; Eric Schickler, "Institutional Change in the House of Representatives, 1867–1998: A Test of Partisan and Ideological Power Balance Models," *American Political Science Review* 94 (2000): 269–88.

62. James L. Sundquist, *The Decline and Resurgence of Congress*, 29.

63. E.E. Schattschneider, *The Semisovereign People: A Realist's View of Democracy in America*, 86.

64. "Asks Moose Votes on Wilson Record," *New York Times*, July 3, 1916, 15.

5 Third Parties and Civic Engagement

1. Bernard R. Berelson, Paul F. Lazerfield, and William N. McPhee, *Voting: A Study of Opinion Formation in a Presidential Campaign* (Chicago, IL: University of Chicago Press, 1954); Angus Campbell, Phillip Converse, Warren Miller, and Donald Stokes, *The American Voter* (New York, Wiley, 1960); Michael X. Delli Carpini, and Scott Keeter, *What Americans Know About Politics and Why it Matters* (New Haven, CT: Yale University Press, 1996); John Zaller, "The Myth of a Massive Media Impact Revisited," in *Political Persuasion and Attitude Change*, eds. Diana C. Mutz, Paul M. Sniderman, and Richard A. Brody (Ann Arbor, MI: University of Michigan Press, 1996).

2. Raymond E. Wolfinger, and Steven J. Rosenstone, *Who Votes?* (New Haven, CT: Yale University Press, 1980); Guy A. Teixeira, *The Disappearing American Voter* (Washington, DC: The Brookings Institute, 1992); Benjamin Highton, and Raymond E. Wolfinger, "The Political Implications of Higher Turnout," *British Journal of Political Science* 31 (2001): 179–223.

3. Both instances, just referenced, are themselves based on normatively questionable assumptions. In the first instance, the candidate who does not want his opponent's

supporters to turn out is acting on a rational but also wholly self-centered basis. In the second instance, the assumption that you cannot trust traditional non-voting populations to make wise decisions must assume that the traditional voting population is making shrewd decisions. Given the low levels of approval and trust of politicians from the two major political parties in the United States, uncovered and discussed in Chapter 1, it seems that people are less than perfectly impressed with the decisions the voting population, to date, has been making.

4. V.O. Key, *Southern Politics in State and Nation* (New York: Vintage Books, 1949), 527.

5. Carole Pateman, *Participation and Democratic Theory* (New York: Cambridge University Press, 1970); Steven Finkel, "The Reciprocal Effects of Participation and Political Efficacy," *American Journal of Political Science* 29 (1985): 891–913.

6. Arend Lijphart, "Unequal Participation: Democracy's Unresolved Dilemma," *American Political Science Review* 91 (1997): 1–14, quote from page 1.

7. It has been found that public services improved at the local level of government for African Americans when this group became more likely to turn out to vote after the passage of the Voting Rights Act of 1965, see James W. Button, *Blacks and Social Change: Impact of the Civil Rights Movement in Southern Communities* (Princeton, NJ: Princeton University Press, 1989); and William R. Keech, *The Impact of Negro Voting: The Role of the Vote in the Quest for Equality* (Chicago, IL: Rand McNally, 1968).

8. Research has found that state spending on welfare is associated with the level of poor citizens who vote, see Kim Quaile Hill, and Jan Leighley, "The Policy Consequences of Class Bias in State Electorates," *American Journal of Political Science* 36 (1992): 351–65; and that voter turnout is linked to state transfers to counties, see Stephen Ansolabehere, Alan Gerber, and James Snyder, "Equal Votes, Equal Money: Court Ordered Redistricting and Public Expenditures in American States," *American Political Science Review* 96 (2002): 767–77.

9. Walter R. Mebane, Jr., "Fiscal Constraints and Electoral Manipulation in American Social Welfare," *American Political Science Review* 88 (1994): 77–94; Paul S. Martin, "Voting's Rewards: Voter Turnout, Attentive Publics, and Congressional Allocation of Federal Money," *American Journal of Political Science* 47 (2003): 110–27.

10. Carole Pateman, *Participation and Democratic Theory.*

11. Charles Merriam, and Harold Gosnell, *Non-Voting: Causes and Methods of Control* (Chicago, IL: University of Chicago Press, 1924); Daniel Katz, and Samuel Elversveld, "The Impact of Local Party Activity upon the Electorate," *Public Opinion Quarterly* 25 (1961): 1–24; Gerald Kramer, "The Effects of Precinct Level Canvassing on Voter Behavior," *Public Opinion Quarterly* 34 (1970): 560–72; Jack Nagel, *Participation* (Englewood Cliffs, NJ: Prenitice Hall, 1987); Kenneth M. Goldstein, and Travis N. Ridout, "The Politics of Participation: Mobilization and Turnout Over Time," *Political Behavior* 24 (2002): 3–29.

12. Samuel Kernell, and Gary Jacobson, *Logic of American Politics* (Washington, DC: Congressional Quarterly Press, 2000), 358. For evidence of the importance of political parties for mobilization in earlier eras, see Daniel Katz, and Samuel Elversveld, "The Impact of Local Party Activity upon the Electorate"; and Gerald Kramer, "The Effects of Precinct Level Canvassing on Voter Behavior."

13. Maine has two Republican United States senators at the time of this writing.

14. Jimmy Carter, the Democratic nominee, boycotts the debate because of Anderson's invitation; see Elaine P. Adams, "Chronology 1980," *Foreign Affairs* 59 (1980): 714–42.

15. Steven J. Rosenstone, Roy L. Behr, and Edward H. Lazarus, *Third Parties in America*, 2nd edition (Princeton, NJ: Princeton University Press, 1996), 238.

16. Surveys of the literature produced in the 20th century can be found in Andre Blais, *To Vote or Not to Vote?* (Pittsburgh, PA: University of Pittsburgh Press, 2000); Kay Lehman Schlozman, "Citizen Participation in America: What Do We Know? Why Do We Care," in *Political Science the State of the Discipline*, eds. Ira Katznelson, and Helen V. Miller (New York: W.W. Norton, 2002).

17. In 1991, John G. Matsusaka counts 25 papers that had been published that test whether people are more likely to vote in close elections, see John G. Matsusaka, "Election Closeness and Voter Turnout: Evidence from California Ballot Propositions," *Public Choice* 76 (1993): 313–34.

18. These elections are chosen because it is not reasonable to presume that third party voting will relate to anything systematic when there are not reasonably salient third party candidates running.

19. Geoffrey C. Layman, and Edward G. Carmines, "Cultural Conflict in American Politics: Religious Traditionalism, Postmaterialism, and U.S. Political Behavior," *The Journal of Politics* 59 (1997): 751–77.

20. Anthony Downs, *An Economic Theory of Democracy* (New York: Harper Collins Publishers, 1957); W.H. Riker, and P.C. Ordeshook, "A Theory of the Calculus of Voting," *American Political Science Review* 62 (1968): 29–54.

21. John G. Matsusaka, "Election Closeness and Voter Turnout: Evidence from California Ballot Propositions."

22. Raymond E. Wolfinger, and Steven J. Rosenstone, *Who Votes?*.

23. See John G. Matsusaka, "Explaining Voter Turnout Patterns: An Information Theory," *Public Choice* 84 (1995): 91–117; Timothy Feddersen, and Wolfgang Pesendorfer, "The Swing Voter's Curse," *American Economic Review* 86 (1996): 408–24.

24. In studies of cross-national variance in voter turnout scholars normally include a measure of literacy in their econometric models.

25. Robert A. Jackson, "A Reassessment of Voter Mobilization," *Political Research Quarterly* 49 (1996): 331–49.

26. Samuel Kernell, "Presidential Popularity and Negative Voting: An Alternative Explanation of the Mid-term Congressional Decline of the President's Party," *American Political Science Review* 71 (1977): 44–66; Kay Lehman Schlozman, and Sidney Verba, *Injury to Insult* (Cambridge, MA: Harvard University Press, 1979).

27. Richard A. Brody, and Paul M. Sniderman, "From Life Space to Polling Place: The Relevance of Personal Concerns for Voting Behavior," *British Journal of Political Science* 7 (1977): 337–60; Harry Maurer, *Not Working: An Oral History of the Unemployed* (New York: Holt, Rinehart, and Winston, 1980).

28. Virginia Gray, and David Lowery, "The Diversity of State Interest Group Systems," *Political Research Quarterly* 46 (1993): 81–97; and Virginia Gray, and David Lowery, "Environmental Limits on the Diversity of State Interest Group Systems: A Population Ecology Interpretation," *Political Research Quarterly* 49 (1996): 103–18.

29. Contention is based on an e-mail exchange with Virginia Gray, University of North Carolina, on September 6, 2010.

30. Other work has called into question the nature of the relationship between the closeness of elections and voter turnout. For example, see C.B. Foster, "The Performance of Rational Voter Models in Recent Presidential Elections," *American Political Science Review* 78 (1984): 678–90; G.W. Cox, "Closeness and Turnout: A Methodological Note," *The Journal of Politics* 50 (1988): 768–75; John G. Matsusaka, and F. Palda, "The Downsian Voter Meets the Ecological Fallacy," paper prepared for the Fraser Institute at the University of Southern California.

31. The coefficient for "Third Party Voting" represents a little more than 2.5 percent, of a one standard deviation change, in the dependent variable, on average, all else being equal.

32. Nathaniel Beck, and Jonathan N. Katz, "What to do (and not to do) with Time-Series Cross-Section Data," *American Political Science Review* 89 (1995): 634–47.

6 How to Make Third Parties Viable Once More?

1. American Political Science Association Committee on Political Parties, "Toward a More Responsible Two-Party System," *American Political Science Review* 44 (1950): 1–3, 18–29; Austin Ranney, and Willmoore Kendall, *Democracy and the American Party System* (New York: Harcourt and Brace, 1956); Nelson W. Polsby, and Aaron Wildavsky, *Presidential Elections: Strategies and Structures in American Politics*, 9th edition (Chatham, NJ: Chatham House, 1996); Steven J. Rosenstone, Roy L. Behr, and Edward H. Lazarus, *Third Parties in America*, 2nd edition (Princeton, NJ: Princeton University Press, 1996), 219–21; Micah L. Sifry, *Spoiling for a Fight: Minor-Party Politics in America* (New York: Routledge, 2002).

2. E.E. Schattschneider, *The Semi-Sovereign People: a Realist's View of Democracy in America* (New York: Holt, Rinehart, and Winston, 1960); Daniel A. Mazmanian, "Moving Outside or Around the Two-Party System: Minor Parties in Presidential Elections," in *Parties and Elections in an Anti-Party Age,* ed. Jeff Fishel (Bloomington, IN: Indiana University Press, 1978); Paul S. Herrnson, "Two-Party Dominance and Minor Party Forays in American Politics," in *Multiparty Politics in American,* eds. Paul S. Herrnson and John C. Green (Lanham, MD: Rowman and Littlefield Publishers, Inc., 1997).

3. John D. Hicks, "The Minor Party Tradition in American Politics," *The Mississippi Valley Historical Review* 20 (1933): 3–28; Theodore J. Lowi, "Toward a More Responsible Three-Party System: The Mythology of the Two Party System and the Prospects for Reform," *PS* 16 (1983): 699–706; Theodore J. Lowi, "Toward a Responsible Three-Party System: Plan or Obituary?" in *The State of the Parties*, eds. John C. Green and Daniel M. Shea (Lanham, MD: Rowman and Littlefield, Inc., 1999); David D. Schmidt, *Citizen Lawmakers: the Ballot Initiative Revolution* (Philadelphia, PA: Temple University Press, 1989); Steven J. Rosenstone, Roy L. Behr, and Edward H. Lazarus, *Third Parties in America*; Shigeo Hirano, and James M. Snyder Jr., "The Decline of Minor-Party Voting in the United States," *Journal of Politics* 69 (2007): 1–16.

4. Shaun Bowler, and David J. Lanoue, "Strategic and Protest Voting for Minor Parties: The Case of the Canadian NDP," *Political Research Quarterly* 45 (1992): 485–99; Geoff Peterson, and J. Mark Wrighton, "Expressions of Distrust: Minor-Party Voting and Cynicism in Government," *Political Behavior* 20 (1998): 17–34; Thomas Stratmann, "Ballot Access Restrictions and Candidate Entry in Elections," *European Journal of Political Economy* 21 (2005): 59–71.

5. Diana Dwyre, and Robin Kolodny, "Barriers to Minor Party Success and Prospects for Change," in *Multiparty Politics in American*, eds. Paul S. Herrnson and John C. Green (Lanham, MD: Rowman and Littlefield Publishers, Inc., 1997); James A. Reichley, "The Future of the American Two-Party System," in *The State of the Parties,* eds. John C. Green, and Daniel M. Shea (Lanham, MD: Rowman and Littlefield, Inc., 1999).

6. Howard P. Nash, *Third Parties in American Politics* (Washington, DC: Public Affairs Press, 1959); Mark Voss-Hubbard, "The 'Third Party Tradition' Reconsidered: Third Parties and American Public Life, 1830–1900," *Journal of American History* 86 (1999): 121–50; Shigeo Hirano, and James M. Snyder Jr., "The Decline of Minor-Party Voting in the United States."

7. Australia uses preferential voting for elections to the House of Representatives and a form of proportional representation for elections to the Senate; both of these

election formats also prompt more viable third political parties. The two largest parties in Australia are the Australian Labour Party and the Liberal Party, the two dominant parties in Ireland are Fiánna Fail and Fine Gael, and the two dominant political parties in Mexico are the National Action Party (PAN) and the Institutional Revolutionary Party (PRI). However, in recent Mexican elections, a third party, the Party of the Democratic Revolution (PRD), has been consistently winning some representation suggesting the country may be moving to a three-party dominant party system.

8. Justin Levitt, and Michael P. McDonald, "Taking the 'Re' out of Redistricting: State Constitutional Provisions on Redistricting Timing," *Georgetown Law Journal* 95 (2007): 1247–85, fn.18.

9. Information is gathered from the national Green Party website and from the various city websites.

10. See Mathew J. Streb, *Rethinking American Electoral Democracy* (London, UK: Taylor and Francis Group, 2008), 71–75.

11. For a work that examines the traditional culture of Southern states see David Elazar, *American Federalism: a View from the States* (New York, NY: Crowell, 1966).

12. See Mathew J. Streb, *Rethinking American Electoral Democracy*, 11–16.

13. Ibid.

14. Brian Frederick, *Congressional Representation & Constituents: The Case for Increasing the U.S. House of Representatives* (London, UK: Taylor and Francis Group, 2008).

References

Abramson, Paul R., John H. Aldrich, Phillip Paolino, and David W. Rohde. "Challenges to the American Two-Party System: Evidence from the 1968, 1980, 1992, and 1996 Presidential Elections." *Political Research Quarterly* 53 (2000): 495–522.

Adams, Greg D. "Legislative Effects of Single-Member vs. Multi-Member Districts." *American Journal of Political Science* 40 (1996): 129–44.

Adams, Elaine P. "Chronology 1980." *Foreign Affairs* 59 (1980): 714–42.

Aldrich, John. "Political Parties in a Critical Era." *American Politics Quarterly* 27 (1999): 9–32.

Aldrich, John H., and David W. Rohde. "The Logic of Conditional Party Government: Revisiting the Electoral Connection." In *Congress Reconsidered*, 7th edition, edited by Lawrence C. Dodd, and Bruce I. Oppenheimer. Washington, DC: CQ Press, 2001.

Allen, Neal, and Brian J. Brox. "The Roots of Third Party Voting: the 2000 Nader Campaign in Historical Perspective." *Party Politics* 11 (2005): 623–37.

Alvarez, Michael R. and Jonathan Nagler. "Economics, Issues and the Perot Candidacy: Voter Choice in the 1992 Presidential Election." *American Journal of Political Science* 39 (1995): 714–44.

American Political Science Association Committee on Political Parties. "Toward a More Responsible Two-Party System." *American Political Science Review* 44 (1950): 1–3, 18–29.

Andrews, Josephine T., and Robert W. Jackman. "If Winning Isn't Everything, Why Do They Keep Score? Consequences of Electoral Performance for Party Leaders." *British Journal of Political Science* 38 (2008): 657–75.

Ansolabehere, Stephen, and Alan Gerber. "The Effects of Filing Fees and Petition Requirements on U.S. House Elections." *Legislative Studies Quarterly* 21 (1996): 249–64.

Ansolabehere, Stephen, Alan Gerber, and James Snyder. "Equal Votes, Equal Money: Court Ordered Redistricting and Public Expenditures in American States." *American Political Science Review* 96 (2002): 767–77.

Argersinger, Peter H. "A Place on the Ballot: Fusion Politics and Antifusion Laws." *American Historical Review* 85 (1980): 289–306.

"Asks Moose Votes on Wilson Record." *New York Times*, July 3, 1916, 15.

Beck, Nathaniel, and Jonathan N. Katz. "What to do (and not to do) with Time-Series Cross-Section Data." *American Political Science Review* 89 (1995): 634–47.

Berelson, Bernard R., Paul F. Lazerfield, and William N. McPhee. *Voting: A Study of Opinion Formation in a Presidential Campaign.* Chicago, IL: University of Chicago Press, 1954.

Berry, William D., Even J. Ringquist, Richard C. Fording, and Russell L. Hanson. "Measuring Citizen and Government Ideology in the American States, 1960–93." *American Journal of Political Science* 42 (1998): 327–48.

Bibby, John F., and L. Sandy Maisel. *Two-Parties-or More?: The American Party System.* Boulder, CO: Westview Press, 2003.

Binder, Sarah A. "The Partisan Basis of Procedural Choice: Allocating Parliamentary Rights in the House, 1789–1991." *American Political Science Review* 90 (1996): 8–20.

———. *Stalemate: Causes and Consequences of Legislative Gridlock, 1947–96.* Washington, DC: Brookings Institute Press, 2003.

Blais, Andre. *To Vote or Not to Vote?.* Pittsburgh, PA: University of Pittsburgh Press, 2000.

Boehlert, Eric. "Al's Ballot Blues." *Open Salon 2000.* Available at http://www.salon.com/news/politics/feature/2000/11/16/ballots/print.html (accessed August 15, 2010).

Book of States. Lexington, KY: Council of State Governments, 2008.

Bowler, Shaun, and David J. Lanoue. "Strategic and Protest Voting for Third Parties: the Case of the Canadian NDP." *The Western Political Quarterly* 45 (1992): 485–99.

———. "New Party Challenges and Partisan Change: The Effects of Party Competition on Party Loyalty." *Political Behavior* 18 (1996): 327–43.

Brady, David W., and Craig Volden. *Revolving Gridlock: Politics and Policy from Carter to Clinton.* Boulder, CO: Westview Press, 1997.

Brody, Richard A., and Paul M. Sniderman. "From Life Space to Polling Place: The Relevance of Personal Concerns for Voting Behavior." *British Journal of Political Science* 7 (1977): 337–60.

Brown, Mark R. "Popularizing Ballot Access: the Front Door to Election Reform." *Ohio State Law Journal* 58 (1997): 1281–324.

Budge, Ian, and Richard I. Hofferbert. "Mandates and Policy Outputs: U.S. Party Platforms and Federal Expenditures." *American Political Science Review* 84 (1990): 111–31.

Burden, Barry C. "Minor Parties and Strategic Voting in Recent U.S. Presidential Elections." *Electoral Studies* 24 (2005): 603–18.

———. "Ballot Regulations and Multiparty Politics in the States." *PS* 40 (2007): 669–73.

Burden, Barry C., and Steven Greene. "Party Attachments and State Election Laws." *Political Research Quarterly* 53 (2000): 63–76.

Button, James W. *Blacks and Social Change: Impact of the Civil Rights Movement in Southern Communities.* Princeton, NJ: Princeton University Press, 1989.

Campbell, Angus, Phillip Converse, Warren Miller, and Donald Stokes. *The American Voter.* New York: Wiley, 1960.

Chace, James. *Wilson, Roosevelt, Taft, and Debs—the Election That Changed the Country.* New York: Simon and Schuster, 2004.

Clancy, Herbert J. *The Presidential Election of 1880.* Chicago, IL: Loyola University Press, 1958.

Clinton, Joshua, and John Lapinski. "Measuring Legislative Accomplishment, 1877–1994." *American Journal of Political Science* 50 (2006): 232–49.

Cobble, Steve, and Sarah Siskind. *Fusion: Multiple Party Nomination in the United States*. Washington, DC: Center for a New Democracy, 2003.

Coleman, John J. "Unified Government, Divided Government, and Party Responsiveness." *American Political Science Review* 93 (1999): 821–35.

Cooper, Joseph. "From Congressional to Presidential Preeminence: Power and Politics in Late Nineteenth-Century America and Today." In *Congress Reconsidered, 9th edition*, edited by Lawrence C. Dodd and Bruce I. Oppenheimer. Washington, DC: Congressional Quarterly Press, 2009.

Cooper, Joseph, and David W. Brady. "Institutional Context and Leadership Style: The House from Cannon to Rayburn." *American Political Science Review* 75 (1981): 411–25.

Cox, G.W. "Closeness and Turnout: A Methodological Note." *Journal of Politics* 50 (1988): 768–75.

Cox, Gary W., and Mathew D. McCubbins. *Setting the Agenda. Responsible Party Government in the US House of Representatives*. Cambridge, UK: Cambridge University Press, 2005.

Dailey, Jane. *Before Jim Crow: The Politics of Race in Postemancipation Virginia*. Chapel Hill, NC: University of North Carolina Press, 2000.

Delli Carpini, Michael X., and Scott Keeter. *What Americans Know About Politics and Why it Matters*. New Haven, CT: Yale University Press, 1996.

De Santis, Vincent P. *Republicans Face the Southern Question: The New Departure Years*. Baltimore, MD: Johns Hopkins Press, 1959.

Disch, Lisa Jane. *The Tyranny of the Two-Party System*. New York: Columbia University Press, 2002.

Dodd, Lawrence C., and Scot Schraufnagel. "Congress, Civility and Legislative Productivity: A Historical Perspective." In *Congress Reconsidered, 9th edition*, edited by Lawrence C. Dodd and Bruce I. Oppenheimer. Washington, DC: Congressional Quarterly Press, 2009.

Downey, Matthew T. "Horace Greeley and the Politicians: The Liberal Republican Convention in 1872." *Journal of American History* 53 (1967): 727–50.

Downs, Anthony. *An Economic Theory of Democracy*. New York: Harper Collins Publishers, 1957.

Dubin, Michael J. *Party Affiliations in the State Legislatures: A Year by Year Summary, 1796–2006*. Jefferson, NC: McFarland and Company, 2007.

Duverger, Maurice. *Political Parties, Their Organization and Activity in the Modern State*. New York: Wiley, 1954.

Dwyre, Diana, and Robin Kolodny. "Barriers to Minor Party Success and Prospects for Change." In *Multiparty Politics in America*, edited by Paul S. Herrnson and John C. Green. Lanham, MD: Rowman and Littlefield Publishers, 1997.

Edwards III, George C., Andrew Barrett, and Jeffrey Peake. "The Legislative Impact of Divided Government." *American Journal of Political Science* 41 (1997): 545–63.

Edwards, Rebecca. *The Silver Party*. Poughkeepsie, NY: Vassar College, 2000.

Elazar, David. *American Federalism: a View from the States*. New York, NY: Crowell, 1966.

Evans, Eldon C. *A History of the Australian Ballot System in the United States*. Chicago, IL: University of Chicago Press, 1917.

Feddersen, Timothy, and Wolfgang Pesendorfer. "The Swing Voter's Curse." *American Economic Review* 86 (1996): 408–24.

Finkel, Steven. "The Reciprocal Effects of Participation and Political Efficacy." *American Journal of Political Science* 29 (1985): 891–913.

Fiorina, Morris P. "Split Party Government in the American States: A Byproduct of Legislative Professionalism." *American Political Science Review* 88 (1994): 304–16.

Foster, C.B. "The Performance of Rational Voter Models in Recent Presidential Elections." *American Political Science Review* 78 (1984): 678–90.

Fredrick, Brian. *Congressional Representation & Constituents: The Case for Increasing the U.S. House of Representatives.* New York: Routledge, 2010.

Gable, John A. *The Bull Moose Years: Theodore Roosevelt and the Progressive Party.* Port Washington, NY: Kenniket Press, 1978.

Gerber, Richard Allen. "The Liberal Republicans of 1872 in Historiographical Perspective." *Journal of American History* 61 (1975): 40–73.

Ginsberg, Benjamin, Theodore J. Lowi, and Margaret Weir. *We the People: An Introduction to American Politics, 2nd edition.* New York: W.W. Norton & Company, 1999.

Glad, Paul W. *The History of Wisconsin, Volume V: War, A New Era, and Depression, 1914–1940.* Madison, WI: Wisconsin State Historical Society Press, 1990.

Glass, Mary Ellen. *Silver and Politics in Nevada: 1892–1902.* Reno, NV: University of Nevada Press, 1969.

Gold, Howard J. "Third Party Voting in Presidential Elections: A Study of Perot, Anderson, and Wallace." *Political Research Quarterly* 48 (1995): 751–73.

Goldsmith, David. *A History of the Maryland Greens: 1990–2003.* San Francisco, CA: Ruby Skye, 2004.

Goldstein, Kenneth M., and Travis N. Ridout. "The Politics of Participation: Mobilization and Turnout Over Time." *Political Behavior* 24 (2002): 3–29.

Goodwyn, Lawrence. *The Populist Movement: A Short History of the Agrarian Revolt in America.* Oxford, UK: Oxford Press, 1978.

Gray, Virginia, and David Lowery. "The Diversity of State Interest Group Systems." *Political Research Quarterly* 46 (1993): 81–97.

——. "Environmental Limits on the Diversity of State Interest group Systems: A Population Ecology Interpretation." *Political Research Quarterly* 49 (1996): 103–18.

Heitschusen, Valerie, and Garry Young. "Macropolitics and Changes in the U.S. Code: Testing Competing Theories of Policy Production, 1874–1946." In *The Macropolitics of Congress,* edited by E. Scott Adler and John S. Lapinski. Princeton, NJ: Princeton University Press, 2006.

Henretta, James A., David Brody, Lynn Dumenil, and Susan Ware. *America's History, 5th edition.* Boston, MA: Bedford/St. Martin, 2004.

Herrnson, Paul. "Two-Party Dominance and Minor Party Forays in American Politics." In *Multiparty Politics in America,* edited by Paul S. Herrnson and John C. Green. Lanham, MD: Rowman and Littlefield Publishers, 1997.

——. "Minor-Party Candidates in Congressional Elections." In *The Marketplace of Democracy: Electoral Competition and American Politics,* edited by Michael P. McDonald and John Samples. Washington DC: Brookings Institution Press, 2006.

Hershey, Marjorie Randon. *Party Politics in America, 12th edition.* New York: Longman Classics, 2007.

Hicks, John D. "The Minor Party Tradition in American Politics." *Mississippi Valley Historical Review* 20 (1933): 3–28.

Highton, Benjamin, and Raymond E. Wolfinger. "The Political Implications of Higher Turnout." *British Journal of Political Science* 31 (2001): 179–223.

Hild, Matthew. *Greenbackers, Knights of Labor, and Populists: Farmer-Labor Insurgency in the Late-nineteenth-century South*. Athens, GA: University of Georgia Press, 2007.

Hill, Kim Quaile, and Jan Leighley. "The Policy Consequences of Class Bias in State Electorates." *American Journal of Political Science* 36 (1992): 351–65.

Hirano, Shigeo, and James M. Snyder, Jr., "The Decline of Third-Party Voting in the United States." *Journal of Politics* 69 (2007): 1–16.

Holsti, Ole R., and James N. Rosenau. "Liberals, Populists, Libertarians, and Conservatives: The Link between Domestic and International Affairs." *International Political Science Review* 17 (1996): 29–54.

Howell, William, Scott Adler, Charles Cameron, and Charles Riemann. "Divided Government and the Legislative Productivity of Congress, 1945–94." *Legislative Studies Quarterly* 25 (2000): 285–312.

Hunt, James L. *Marion Butler and American Populism*. Chapel Hill, NC: University of North Carolina Press, 2003.

Hurley, Patricia A. "Assessing the Potential for Significant Legislative Output in the House of Representatives." *Western Political Quarterly* 32 (1979): 45–58.

Jackson, Robert A. "A Reassessment of Voter Mobilization." *Political Research Quarterly* 49 (1996): 331–49.

Jacobson, Gary C. *The Politics of Congressional Elections, 6th edition*. New York: Longman, 2004.

Jewell, Malcolm E. *Parties and Primaries*. New York: Praeger Publishers, 1984.

Jones, David R. "Party Polarization and Legislative Gridlock." *Political Research Quarterly* 54 (2001): 125–41.

Kamieniecku, Sheldon. "The Dimensionality of Partisan Strength and Political Independence." *Political Behavior* 10 (1988): 364–76.

Kasparek, Jonathon. *Fighting Son: A Biography of Philip F. La Follette*. Madison, WI: Wisconsin Historical Society Press, 2006.

Katz, Daniel, and Samuel Elversveld. "The Impact of Local Party Activity upon the Electorate." *Public Opinion Quarterly* 25 (1961): 1–24.

Kazin, Michael. *The Populist Persuasion: An American History*. New York: Basic Books, 1995.

Keech, William R. *The Impact of Negro Voting: The Role of the Vote in the Quest for Equality*. Chicago, IL: Rand McNally, 1968.

Kelly, Sean Q. "Divided We Govern: A Reassessment." *Polity* 25 (1993): 475–84.

Kernell, Samuel. "Presidential Popularity and Negative Voting: An Alternative Explanation of the Mid-term Congressional Decline of the President's Party." *American Political Science Review* 71 (1977): 44–66.

Kernell, Samuel, and Gary Jacobson. *Logic of American Politics*. Washington, DC: Congressional Quarterly Press, 2000.

Key, V.O. *Southern Politics in State and Nation*. New York: Vintage Books, 1949.

Kingdom, John. "Models of Legislative Voting." *Journal of Politics* 39 (1977): 563–95.

Kramer, Gerald. "The Effects of Precinct Level Canvassing on Voter Behavior." *Public Opinion Quarterly* 34 (1970): 560–72.

Krehbiel, Keith. "Institutional and Partisan Sources of Gridlock: A Theory of Divided and Unified Government." *Journal of Theoretical Politics* 8 (1996): 7–40.

Lacy, Dean, and Quin Monson. "The Origins and Impact of Votes for Third-Party Candidates: A Case Study of the 1998 Minnesota Gubernatorial Election." *Political Research Quarterly*, 55 (2002): 409–37.

La Forte, Robert S. "Theodore Roosevelt's Osawatomie Speech." *Kansas Historical Quarterly* 32 (1966): 187–200.

Layman, Geoffrey C., and Edward G. Carmines. "Cultural Conflict in American Politics: Religious Traditionalism, Postmaterialism, and U.S. Political Behavior." *Journal of Politics* 59 (1997): 751–77.

Levitt, Justin, and Michael P. McDonald. "Taking the 'Re' out of Redistricting: State Constitutional Provisions on Redistricting Timing." *Georgetown Law Journal* 95 (2007): 1247–85.

Lewis-Beck, Michael S., and Peverill Squire. "The Politics of Institutional Choice: Presidential Ballot Access for Third Parties in the United States." *British Journal of Political Science* 25 (1995): 419–27.

Lijphart, Arend. "Unequal Participation: Democracy's Unresolved Dilemma." *American Political Science Review* 91 (1997): 1–14.

Long, J. Scott. *Regression Models for Categorical and Limited Dependent Variable.* Thousand Oaks, CA: Sage Publications, 1997.

Lowi, Theodore J. "Toward a More Responsible Three-Party System: The Mythology of the Two Party System and the Prospects for Reform." *PS* 16 (1983): 699–706.

——. "Toward a Responsible Three-Party System: Plan or Obituary?" In *The State of the Parties*, edited by John C. Green and Daniel M. Shea. Lanham, MD: Rowman and Littlefield Publishers, 1999.

Martin, Paul S. "Voting's Rewards: Voter Turnout, Attentive Publics, and Congressional Allocation of Federal Money." *American Journal of Political Science* 47 (2003): 110–27.

Marquez, Myriam. "Want to Live in a True Democracy? Vote for Open Elections." *Orlando Sentinel*, September 14, 1998, A12.

Matsusaka, John G. "Election Closeness and Voter Turnout: Evidence from California Ballot Propositions." *Public Choice* 76 (1993): 313–34.

——. "Explaining Voter Turnout Patterns: An Information Theory." *Public Choice* 84 (1995): 91–117.

Matsusaka, John G., and F. Palda. "The Downsian Voter Meets the Ecological Fallacy." Paper prepared for the Fraser Institute at the University of Southern California.

Maurer, Harry. *Not Working: An Oral History of the Unemployed.* New York: Holt, Rinehart, and Winston, 1980.

Mayhew, David R. *Divided We Govern: Party Control, Lawmaking, and Investigations, 1946–1990.* New Haven, CT: Yale University Press, 1991.

Mazmanian, Daniel A. *Third Parties in Presidential Elections.* Washington, DC: Brookings Institution, 1974.

——. "Moving Outside or Around the Two-Party System: Minor Parties in Presidential Elections." In *Parties and Elections in an Anti-Party Age*, edited by Jeff Fishel. Bloomington, IN: Indiana University Press, 1978.

McDonald, John F., and Robert A. Moffitt. "The Uses of Tobit Analysis." *Review of Economics and Statistics* 62 (1980): 318–21.

Mebane Jr., Walter R. "Fiscal Constraints and Electoral Manipulation in American Social Welfare." *American Political Science Review* 88 (1994): 77–94.

Merriam, Charles, and Harold Gosnell. *Non-Voting: Causes and Methods of Control.* Chicago, IL: University of Chicago Press, 1924.

Mink, Gwendolyn. *New Immigration in American Political Development; Union, Party, and State, 1875–1920.* Ithaca, NY: Cornell University Press, 1986.

Mowry, George Edwin. *Theodore Roosevelt and the Progressive Movement.* New York: Hill and Wang, 1960.

Nagel, Jack. *Participation.* Englewood Cliffs, NJ: Prentice Hall, 1987.

Nash, Howard P. *Third Parties in American Politics.* Washington, DC: Public Affairs Press, 1959.

Norpoth, Helmut. "Explaining Party Cohesion in Congress: The Case of Shared Policy Attitudes." *American Political Science Review* 70 (1976): 1156–71.

Norrander, Barbara. "Explaining Cross-State Variation in Independent Identification." *American Journal of Political Science* 33 (1989): 516–36.

O'Neil, Deborah. "Third Parties Push for Equal Access to Ballot." *St. Petersburg Times,* August 3, 1998.

Parker, Glenn R. *Congress and the Rent-Seeking Society.* Ann Arbor, MI: University of Michigan Press, 1996.

Pateman, Carole. *Participation and Democratic Theory.* New York: Cambridge University Press, 1970.

Pearson, Charles Chilton. *The Readjuster Movement in Virginia.* New Haven, CT: Yale University Press, 1969.

Peffer, William Alfred. *Populism, Its Rise and Fall.* Lawrence, KS: University Press of Kansas, 1992.

Perez, Robert. "Polling Sites Could Get Crowded." *Orlando Sentinel,* November 12, 1998.

Peterson, Geoff, and J. Mark Wrighton. "Expressions of Distrust: Third-Party Voting and Cynicism in Government." *Political Behavior* 20 (1998): 17–34.

Pinchot, Amos. *History of the Progressive Party, 1912–1916.* New York: New York University Press, 1958.

Polsby, Nelson W., and Aaron Wildavsky. *Presidential Elections: Strategies and Structures in American Politics, 9th edition.* Chatham, NJ: Chatham House, 1996.

Poole, Keith. "Data Download." University of Georgia. Available at http://www. voteview.com/dwnl.htm (last accessed September 3, 2010).

Poole, Keith, and Howard Rosenthal. *Congress: A Political-Economic History of Roll Call Voting.* New York: Oxford University Press, 1997.

Ranney, Austin. *The Doctrine of Responsible Party Government: Its Origins and Present State.* Urbana, IL: The University of Illinois Press, 1954.

Ranney, Austin, and Willmoore Kendall. *Democracy and the American Party System.* New York: Harcourt and Brace, 1956.

Reichley, James A. "The Future of the American Two-Party System." In *The State of the Parties,* edited by John C. Green, and Daniel M. Shea. Lanham, MD: Rowman and Littlefield, Inc., 1999.

Riker, William H. "The Number of Political Parties: A Reexamination of Duverger's Law." *Comparative Politics* 9 (1976): 93–106.

Riker, W.H., and P.C. Ordeshook. "A Theory of the Calculus of Voting." *American Political Science Review* 62 (1968): 29–54.

Robeck, Bruce W., and James A. Dyer. "Ballot Access Requirements in Congressional Elections." *American Politics Research* 10 (1982): 31–45.

Rohde, David. *Parties and Leaders in the Postreform House*. Chicago, IL: University of Chicago Press, 1991.

Roneck, Dennis W. "Learning More from Tobit Coefficients: Extending a Comparative Analysis of Political Protest." *American Sociological Review* 57 (1992): 503–07.

Rosenkranz, Joshua E. "Voter Choice '96: A 50 State Report Card on the Presidential Elections." Brennan Center for Justice at New York University School of Law, 1996.

Rosenstone, Steven J., Roy L. Behr, and Edward H. Lazarus. *Third Parties in America, 2nd edition*. Princeton, NJ: Princeton University Press, 1996.

Ross, Earle Dudley. *The Liberal Republican Movement*. New York: Henry Holt and Company, 1919.

Scarrow, Howard A. "Duverger's Law, Fusion, and the Decline of American 'Third' Parties." *Western Political Quarterly* 39 (1986): 634–47.

Schattschneider, E.E. *The Semisovereign People: A Realist's View of Democracy in America*. New York: Holt, Rinehart, and Winston, Inc, 1960.

Schickler, Eric. "Institutional Change in the House of Representatives, 1867–1998: A Test of Partisan and Ideological Power Balance Models." *American Political Science Review* 94 (2000): 269–88.

Schlozman, Kay Lehman. "Citizen Participation in America: What Do We Know? Why Do We Care?" In *Political Science the State of the Discipline*, edited by Ira Katznelson, and Helen V. Miller. New York: W.W. Norton, 2002.

Schlozman, Kay Lehman, and Sidney Verba. *Injury to Insult*. Cambridge, MA: Harvard University Press, 1979.

Schmidt, David D. *Citizen Lawmakers: The Ballot Initiative Revolution*. Philadelphia, PA: Temple University Press, 1989.

Schraufnagel, Scot, and Jeffery J. Mondak. "The Issue Positions of House Democrats and Republicans: A Research Note." *Political Science Quarterly* 117 (2002): 479–90.

"Senate Passes Currency Bill." *New York Times*, February 16, 1900, 1.

Sifry, Micah L., *Spoiling for a Fight: Minor-Party Politics in America*. New York: Routledge, 2002.

Sinclair, Barbara. *Unorthodox Lawmaking: New Legislative Processes in the U.S. Congress*. Washington, DC: CQ Press, 1997.

Smallwood, Frank. *The Other Candidates: Third Parties in Presidential Elections*. Hanover, NH: University Press of New England, 1983.

Smith, Steven S., and Gerald Gamm. "The Dynamics of Party Government in Congress." In *Congress Reconsidered, 9th edition*, edited by Lawrence C. Dodd and Bruce I. Oppenheimer. Washington, DC: Congressional Quarterly Press, 2009.

Sommerville, Richard, and Christina Clemenson. "Improving Ballot Access in Florida," Green Party of Florida, 1998. Available at http://www.greens.org/s-r/17/17–05.html (last accessed August 15, 2010).

Stata Corporation. "Xttobit: Random Effects Tobit Models." Available at http://www.stata.com/help.cgi?quadchk (last accessed August 12, 2010).

Stratmann, Thomas. "Ballot Access Restrictions and Candidate Entry in Elections." *European Journal of Political Economy* 21 (2005): 59–71.

Streb, Mathew J. *Rethinking American Electoral Democracy*. London, UK: Taylor & Francis Group, 2008.

Sullivan, John L., and Eric M. Uslaner. "Congressional Behavior and Electoral Marginality." *American Journal of Political Science* 22 (1978): 536–53.

Sundquist, James L. *The Decline and Resurgence of Congress*. Washington, DC: The Brookings Institute Press, 1981.

Tamas, Bernard, and Matthew Hindman. "Do State Election Laws Really Hurt Third Parties? Ballot Access, Fusion and Elections to the U.S. House of Representatives." Paper presented at the Midwest Political Science Association, Chicago, IL, 2007.

Teixeira, Ruy A. *The Disappearing American Voter*. Washington, DC: The Brookings Institute Press, 1992.

Unger, Irwin. *The Greenback Era: A Social and Political History of American Finance, 1865–1879*, Princeton, NJ: Princeton University Press, 1964.

Voss-Hubbard, Mark. "The 'Third Party Tradition' Reconsidered: Third Parties and American Public Life, 1830–1900." *Journal of American History* 86 (1999): 121–50.

"Wilson Kept Pledges." *New York Times*, August 30, 1916, 5.

Winger, Richard. "Ballot Access: Good Bills Die." *Ballot Access News*, Volume 12, Number 2 (1996).

——. "Institutional Obstacles to a Multiparty System." In *Multiparty Politics in America*, edited by Paul S. Herrnson and John C. Green. Lanham, MD: Rowman and Littlefield Publishers, 1997.

——. "Maryland Bill Signed." *Ballot Access News*, Volume 14, Number 3 (1998).

——. "Florida Voters Wipe Out Mandatory Petitions." *Ballot Access News*, Volume 14, Number 8 (1998).

Wolfinger, Raymond E., and Steven J. Rosenstone. *Who Votes?* New Haven, CT: Yale University Press, 1980.

Wright, Gerald C., Robert S. Erikson, and John P. McIver. "Measuring State Partisanship and Ideology with Survey Data." *The Journal of Politics* 47 (1985): 469–89.

Zaller, John. "The Myth of a Massive Media Impact Revisited." In *Political Persuasion and Attitude Change*, edited by Diana C. Mutz, Paul M. Sniderman, and Richard A Brody. Ann Arbor, MI: University of Michigan Press, 1996.

Index